Couches and Conversations

A Modern Day Look At How To Implement Inner
Healing Work and Its Relevance Today

Samaria M Colbert

1

The Book: Couches and Conversations

Scripture quotations are from the Holy Bible. The New King James Version: Containing the Old and New Testaments. Nashville TN: Thomas Nelson, 1985. The Message bible: Eugene H. Peterson, 2002. New American Standard Bible

Table Of Contents:

Preface:

God wants His people healed, whole and set free. As a body of believers, we have come to learn and be more aware of the need for healing workers in the counseling field. It is my opinion that although the body of Christ is more aware of inner healing work and what it is, we need clarity, understanding, and wisdom of how to execute and administrate this kind of healing ministry. Healing ministry is not just someone laying hands on your physical ailment. It is also the work of the counselor, who is being used by God to do the work of Christ. That is to heal the broken-hearted.

Isaiah 61 tells us that one of the primary missions of Christ Jesus was to bind up the brokenhearted, to proclaim liberty to the captives, and to set free from prison those who are bound.

A broken heart is not a physical heart condition; it is an emotional, mental condition. When the scripture talks about captives, it wasn't just referring to people in physical prisons. The scripture is referring to emotional, mental and spiritual captivity. This is the work of the counselor.

I believe the Lord commissioned me to write this book because we need a greater understanding of what inner healing is and what inner healing is not. I have said it many times, and as a warning, I will say this repeatedly throughout the book, you must be properly trained, appointed, and called to do this kind of healing work or you will leave someone more damaged and emotional torn. This book is the first of a series that will include several workbooks. It is meant to give you an understanding of inner healing work, and the differences between mental health counseling, inner healing and deliverance ministry. Although they are different, they are all components of the counseling, healing ministry. A spirit led counselor must be well versed, trained to conduct all three.

I believe the unfortunate thing about inner healing work, is that many go through a six-week course or less to be a part of an inner healing ministry within the body of Christ with minimal to no training. Then the church leaders send them off to conduct small groups and counsel people. I have over 12 years' experience in the counseling field and have studied the counseling mental health field for almost twenty years. There is no way this should be allowed in the church. Just like if you want to be a lawyer you have to go to law school, if you want to be a doctor you must go to medical school. If you want to be a counselor, you must be trained.

These series will not give you all the training you need; it is a supplement to the training you should already have. It will go into the details about the specifics of inner healing work.

The first in this series is this book that will break down the principles of inner healing. The other series will include training manuals, group workbooks for small groups, an individual journal, and workbook for the counselees. Also I will be offering, training and teaching seminars all over the country, to train LICENSED mental health counselors, psychologist, Christian counselors and Christian leaders who **ALREADY HAVE A BACKGROUND, FORMAL TRAINING, OR LICENSURE IN THE COUNSELING FIELD.**

A <u>coach or consultant</u> should not treat psychological or mental health issues that should be addressed by a trained counselor. No, you are not going to be able to take one class or get a six-week certificate and be fully trained to treat deep-

seated psychological issues whether you are Christian or not. That is why we therapist/clinicians/counselors get master's degrees and doctorates in the counseling field. Don't think you can cheat the process. Counseling is a ministry that takes YEARS to prepare for like any other ministry.

Yes, I did just put all that in bold. These series of training are meant to be an addition to the training you already have, a stepping stone, **NOT** a onetime only training. You will not be able to finish either training and then be able to say you are a counselor who does this work.

In fact, I was recently accepted into a program at the state level, where I have to go through a year of training to get another level of certification in working with traumatized children. To even apply or get accepted into the program, you had to have a master's degree, be fully licensed and have formidable years of working with the population. Again the training I will be going through is a supplement, and another level of training certification to the years of experience I already have. So will my training. This book will be the first in a series of teachings.

We need a true understanding of all forms of counseling from the standpoint of the Bible. Go with me; I promise you won't be disappointed that you came. We are ready and willing to work in the healing ministry and continue the work that Jesus came to earth to do.

<u>**WARNING**</u>: ALTHOUGH WE ARE WELL AWARE THAT MANY CHRISTIAN MINISTERS CONDUCT COUNSELING SESSIONS OVER THE PHONE.

THE FOLLOWING RESOURCE IS FOR THOSE WHO SEE COUNSELEES IN AN OFFICE SETTING <u>ONLY</u>. IT IS THE AUTHORS EXPERIENCE THAT INNER HEALING SESSIONS PARTICULARLY FOR INDIVIDUALS RECOVERING FROM DEEP PSYCHOLOGICAL ISSUES, SEXUAL ABUSE, OR RAPE NOT BE COMPLETED OVER THE PHONE AND BE COMPLETED IN AN OFFICE BASED OR FACE TO FACE SETTING ONLY. DUE TO THE INTENSE NATURE OF MANY OF THE SESSIONS. WE DO NOT SUPPORT OR ENDORSE INNER HEALING, DELIVERANCE WORK TO BE COMPLETED OVER THE PHONE IN ANY CAPACITY.

Dedicated to all the persons that have been anointed, called and chosen by the Father to the healing ministry of the counselor. May you be commissioned in a greater way, and endowed by the Holy Spirit to a greater capacity upon reading this book.

And to the many individuals that I serve in counseling ministry every day. May you be healed, be made whole and set free in Jesus name.

Thank you for trusting me with your hurts, pains and truth. I am humbled by your strength.

Amen

Disclaimer:

Samaria Colbert is a licensed therapist. She does strictly adhere HIPPA laws that govern confidentiality and Tarasoff laws; with the exception of intent to harm of oneself or another. With that being said, in this book, the author does not release anything confidential or disclose any identifying information about any of the clients she has treated past, present, or future.

This book is not intended to be used as a diagnostic tool, to treat a person with a mental illness. It is simply a healing tool that God is using to bring about emotional healing. It is understood that by no means is this book meant to replace the time and necessity for an individual, group, or family to seek out a licensed mental health counselor and other psychiatric services.

The author is adamant that you contact your local mental health company to seek outpatient therapy and psychiatric services from a licensed mental health professional, NOT your pastor alone.

Chapter 1

What Is Inner Healing?

Isaiah 61:1-2

The Spirit of the Lord God is upon me because; He has anointed me to preach good tidings unto to the meek; He has sent me to bind up the broken hearted, to proclaim liberty to the captive and the opening of the prisons to them that are bound.

If there is one thing that we can agree on that is this world is hurting. In our nation, we are hurting, emotionally, spiritually and physically. Hurt people hurt people. It has long been my belief that the Bible through Jesus Christ has all the knowledge and power we need to heal our world. If we first do not understand this foundational truth that Christ is the answer, then our world is doomed Christian and non-Christian alike.

God has commissioned us as a body of believers not only be hearers of His word but doers. What happens if we the body of Christ never step up and operate as kingdom citizens who have power, and authority to govern the earth? When I was a kid, I was raised in a church where we were taught to be rapture ready. Meaning once you got saved and filled with the Holy Spirit, you lived holy and tried not to sin to make it to heaven. I had never heard of pursuing God's purpose for my life until I went away to college. Imagine the pure excitement when I learned that not only did I have a purpose for being placed on earth, but that God would use me for His glory to bring healing to others.

I am not here to merely talk about how God can usee me, but how He can and will use you. I had also thought that ministry was a church thing. Meaning people in ministry were those behind a pulpit preaching and declaring the word of God. Don't get me wrong that is ministry, but I later learned that God was not limited to a Sunday morning shout or a Wednesday night bible study. I learned that ministry was not only in the church but outside the church as well.

In fact many years ago, I had a dream, in the dream, I was preaching and prophesying very powerfully inside of the church, then the dream shift and there I was preaching and declaring the word of the Lord outside of the church. God was telling me that my ministry was not just in the church, for church folks but for those who are hurting outside of the church. When we think of people having a ministry outside of the church, we almost always assume that there must be something wrong with that. We often think about the compromising Christian artist who has watered down their music so much that you can't tell whether or not they are singing to Jesus or their lover. Or we think of the movie maker, the actress or actor, the entrepreneur who says they are a Christian, but appear to be lukewarm at best. This book is not about entrepreneurship. I believe that God is raising up a body of believers called the remnant who will operate very strongly in all areas of ministry that includes the seven mountains of God, government, arts, entertainment, business, real-estate, the music industry and the human services field without compromise or watering down the gospel in order to gain followers or to be relevant.

Think about it, Jesus ate among sinner, healed the sick, raised the dead, and hung around some questionable characters, but He never compromised the gospel to do be relevant. He never compromised the word of God. He never let sin off the hook. Jesus was an example that we can be uncompromising, not wavering in our faith and still impact the masses. In fact, although according to the scripture we only see Jesus speaking at one church, we read in the text found in Isaiah 61 about His mission and assignment. Him speaking at one church caused great controversy.

Jesus spoke all over a nation and attracted masses of people. He didn't need a church platform or the confirmation of the church to begin His ministry. God the Father confirmed Him when He was baptized in the Jordan river; God said, "this is my son in whom I am well pleased." Matthew 3:17, it teaches us that when God is ready to release you, you don't need the approval of man, God has already confirmed you. Ironically Jesus ministry and ordination never happened inside of a church.

I am not suggesting that we do away with the church not be led or trained by our church leaders. I am saying that it is ultimately God's decision to birth you out when He is ready, you will know it and so will others around you. You may not be at the baptismal pool and have God speak over you like Jesus.

Nevertheless, you will have the oil of anointing on you in such as way and the dove of the Holy Spirit rest upon your life; it will be undeniable that God has confirmed you.

Believe it or not, this does relate to inner healing.

Inner healing first and foremost is a ministry founded by God the Father. It was one of the primary reasons why Jesus Christ came to earth and why God sent Him. Inner healing ministry has existed from the very beginning of time. When Jesus came, His mission was to reinstate what already was. Meaning Jesus didn't create a new form of healing ministry, He simply by executive order of God the Father carried out the full scope of this ministry.

Inner healing simply means to heal the inner man. Let's us go back to Isaiah 61, which tells us why Jesus was sent to earth. I am going to put the same scripture in two different translations, so we have clarity. I want you to notice the words that I have underlined. I will explain further as we go along.

Isaiah 61:1-2 (KJV)

The Spirit of the Lord God is upon me because; He has anointed me to preach good tidings unto to the meek; He has sent me to bind up the broken hearted, to proclaim liberty to the captive and the opening of the prisons to them that are bound.

Isaiah 61:1-2Living Bible (TLB)

61 The Spirit of the Lord God is upon me, because the Lord has anointed me to bring good news to the suffering and afflicted. He has sent me to comfort the brokenhearted, to announce liberty to captives, and to open the eyes of the blind.

2 He has sent me to tell those who mourn that the time of God's favor to them has come, and the day of his wrath to their enemies.

The first thing I must point out is that when the scripture says "broken hearted." He clearly was not limited to individuals who have a heart condition or suffered a heart attack. When the scripture says the broken-hearted, it was referring to an emotional, mental deficit. You can't see a broken heart, you feel it. When your heart is broken you know it. This in essence is the work of the counselor, who uses the strategy of inner healing.

I must pause and reiterate that counseling is a ministry. It is under the scope of the healing ministry. We read Christ mission, but often when we think healing ministry, we think of an individual who has an anointing to heal physical ailments, we don't think of healing ministry under the scope of an emotional, mental issue. We read that the primary mission of Jesus Christ was to heal the broken heart. Let read the scripture further. He also came to proclaim liberty to the captive. Clearly scripture was not limited to someone who is a prison in a physical jail. A captive is a prison, someone bound, enslaved and confined. When a person is suffering from any mental or emotional deficit they are bound, they are enslaved, there is a stronghold, that is invisible but very real.

My question is why does the body of Christ not see the work of the counselor as a healing a ministry? I believe that we don't consider inner healing work to be a ministry as we should. Yes, the body of Christ as a whole has embraced it, but not like we should. Often Christians who are experiencing mental and emotional deficit are forced to seek traditional help from secular counselors, and non-Christian workers, because we don't embrace the inner healing ministry as we should. Or the church may have an inner healing ministry primarily Christian workers who are untrained, not licensed or very ill-equipped to fully to do the work that this kind of healing ministry demands.

If you are not called, equipped and TRAINED properly, you will severely damage people, more so. Meaning someone could leave your office worse off than they came because you have not followed the proper protocol to begin to do this kind of work. Counseling ministry is not for the faint at heart, or the naive person that wants to start an inner healing ministry with no knowledge. Having zeal means nothing if you are not properly trained, called, anointed and appointed for the position. I have written many books, and in most of them, I talk about the preparation and process an individual must go through before God birthed them into ministry. It is the same with the ministry of the counselor you must be processed and prepared before you go into this ministry. Most of the inner healing ministries in traditional churches don't have people that have been processed, prepared and trained. You can't-do this kind of work after getting a six-week or a six-month certificate.

I am a licensed mental health therapist. I have been in the mental health field for almost 12 years now. I have worked in many different capacities, such as case management, in psychiatric hospitals, in a call center for mental health managed care. I have been working as a therapist in the field for the last few years. I can tell you no matter the environment that I have worked in it was Christ who made the difference. It was His anointing on my life that made me a great counselor. What I have learned is that there is still such a need for trained professionals to begin to operate in inner healing ministry like never before.

So what is the alternative? What is the answer? I believe there are no problems without an answer. God provided the answer before we knew there was a problem.

Their answer is the spirit led, properly trained, processed, anointed and appointed licensed counselor.

There are three different aspects of the healing ministry of the counselor. Each of them has their level of training, proper preparation, and processing. See the attached diagram.

Mental Health

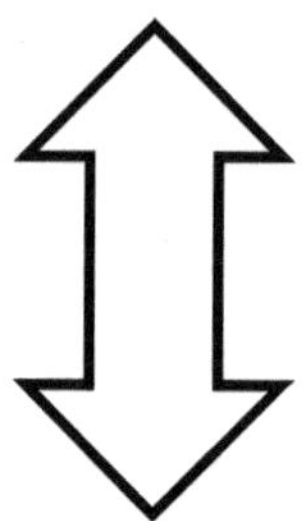

Inner Healing

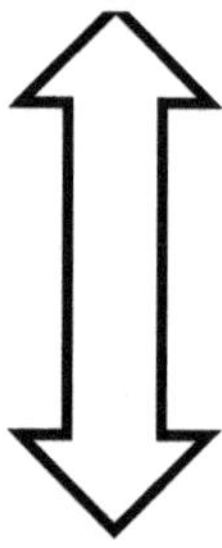

Deliverance

You will notice in the first diagram the arrows are going up and down. The three different avenues of the ministry of the counselor are NOT meant to be the order of treatment or service. Sometimes you have to start at deliverance, other times you start at mental health counseling, you may start right at inner healing. This is where the counselor must you wisdom and discernment.

Mental Health Counseling

Inner Healing

Deliverance

This book focuses primarily on the inner healing part of the counseling ministry. I have several other books that focus on mental health counseling, books such as; The Process Of Emotional Healing, No Fear, Deliverance From Depression, Psychological Warfare. All books address mental illness from a Christian perspective.

Again one must be trained and processed to do mental health counseling; it is again not for the faint at heart. The average mental health counselor can spend up to 6 to 10 years studying and preparing to be a mental health counselor.

Mental health counseling primary deals with the disease of mental illness and symptoms. Then there is deliverance ministry. I won't talk much about this ministry aspect because there is so much knowledge about deliverance ministry. Deliverance ministry is simply the casting out of demons. I do have a book entitled; Demons, Deliverance and Spiritual Warfare that you may want to pick up.

Again an individual does not want to start doing deliverance ministry just because they feel like it. One must be properly called, anointed and appointed to deliverance ministry. You must without a doubt have a real strong relationship with Christ, or you will end up like the Sons of Sceva. This is serious folks very serious. In fact to reiterate my point lets read the story of the Sons of Sceva.

Acts 19:11-16Living Bible (TLB)

11 And God gave Paul the power to do unusual miracles,

12 so that even when his handkerchiefs or parts of his clothing were placed upon sick people, they were healed, and any demons within them came out.

13 A team of itinerant Jews who were traveling from town to town casting out demons planned to experiment by using the name of the Lord Jesus. The incantation they decided on was this: "I adjure you by Jesus, whom Paul preaches, to come out!"

14 Seven sons of Sceva, a Jewish priest, were doing this.

15 But when they tried it on a man possessed by a demon, the demon replied, "I know Jesus and I know Paul, but who are you?"

16 And he leaped on two of them and beat them up, so that they fled out of his house naked and badly injured.

Don't start out in ministry until God has released you. Scripture tells us to not lay hands on anyone suddenly.

1 Timothy 5:22 (KJV)

22 Lay hands suddenly on no man, neither be partaker of other men's sins: keep thyself pure.

The reason why you shouldn't be so quick to jump into ministry is because you are only covered when God has released you. When you operate in ministry before your time, you can be potentially a victim of your own demise. Remember spirits transfer you won't be able to remain pure operating in ministry before the time of release.

Look what happened, after Jesus trained and developed His disciples.

Luke 10:1-17Living Bible (TLB)

1 The Lord now chose seventy other disciples and sent them on ahead in pairs to all the towns and villages he planned to visit later.

2 These were his instructions to them: "Plead with the Lord of the harvest to send out more laborers to help you, for the harvest is so plentiful and the workers so few.

3 Go now, and remember that I am sending you out as lambs among wolves.

 4 Don't take any money with you, or a beggar's bag, or even an extra pair of shoes. And don't waste time along the way.[a]

5 "Whenever you enter a home, give it your blessing.

 6 If it is worthy of the blessing, the blessing will stand; if not, the blessing will return to you.

7 "When you enter a village, don't shift around from home to home, but stay in one place, eating and drinking without question whatever is set before you. And don't hesitate to accept hospitality, for the workman is worthy of his wages!

8-9 "If a town welcomes you, follow these two rules:

(1) Eat whatever is set before you.

(2) Heal the sick; and as you heal them, say, 'The Kingdom of God is very near you now.'

10 "But if a town refuses you, go out into its streets and say,

11 'We wipe the dust of your town from our feet as a public announcement of your doom. Never forget how close you were to the Kingdom of God!'

12 Even wicked Sodom will be better off than such a city on the Judgment Day.

13 What horrors await you, you cities of Chorazin and Bethsaida! For if the miracles I did for you had been done in the cities of Tyre and Sidon,[b] their people would have sat in deep repentance long ago, clothed in sackcloth and throwing ashes on their heads to show their remorse.

14 Yes, Tyre and Sidon will receive less punishment on the Judgment Day than you.

15 And you people of Capernaum, what shall I say about you? Will you be exalted to heaven? No, you shall be brought down to hell."

16 Then he said to the disciples, "Those who welcome you are welcoming me. And those who reject you are rejecting me. And those who reject me are rejecting God who sent me."

17 When the seventy disciples returned, they joyfully reported to him, "Even the demons obey us when we use your name."

You will notice that first Jesus sends His disciples off. I want to put special emphasis on His disciples. A disciple is a student, a follower. You can be a student or follower of anyone and any school of thought. However, Jesus never sent off anyone who first didn't belong to Him and whom he first hadn't discipled, which means to teach or be taught. It is the same today if you haven't been schooled, discipled you are not qualified to do inner healing work. You must have been a disciple of Jesus first studied and learned the craft of the healing ministry of Christ.

Then Jesus gave them divine instructions, with the instruction, came warning. He also gave them the authority to heal, and authority over demons. That is a vast difference from the sons of Sceva they had the position and the title of itinerant ministers but no permission, authority from God. This is very important when it comes to inner healing ministry, and the work of the Christ led counselor.

First, we will define what inner healing counseling ministry is? It is simply through the ministry of the counselor we are peeling back the layers and getting to the root. I call this the onion.

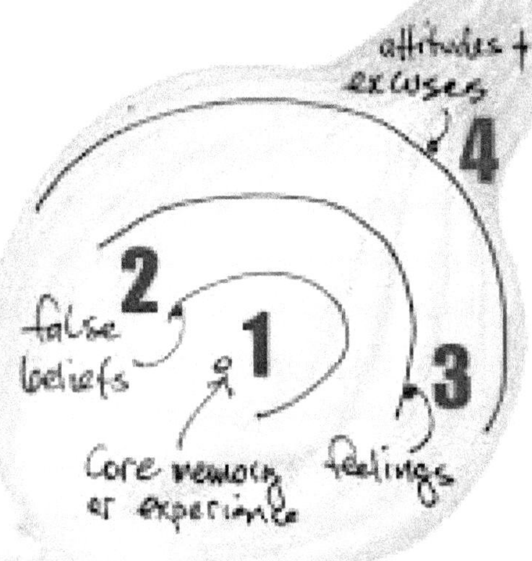

5 habits + behaviors
attitudes + excuses
4
2
false beliefs
1
3
Core memory or experience
feelings

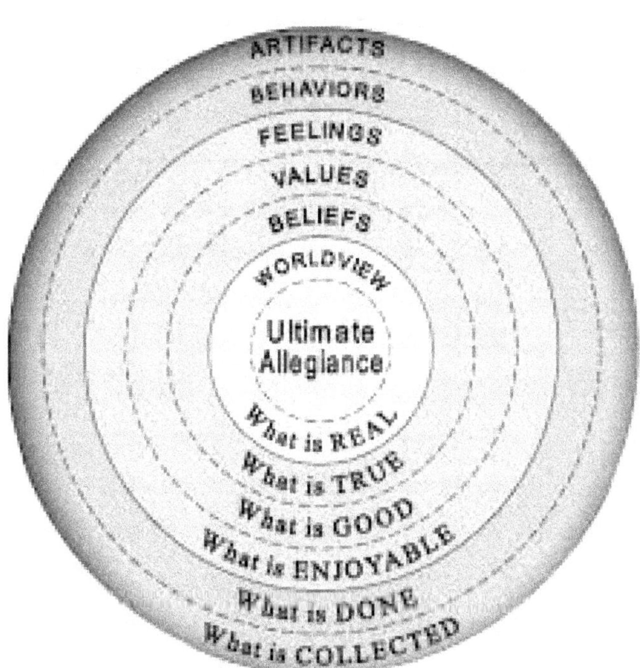

ARTIFACTS
BEHAVIORS
FEELINGS
VALUES
BELIEFS
WORLDVIEW
Ultimate Allegiance
What is REAL
What is TRUE
What is GOOD
What is ENJOYABLE
What is DONE
What is COLLECTED

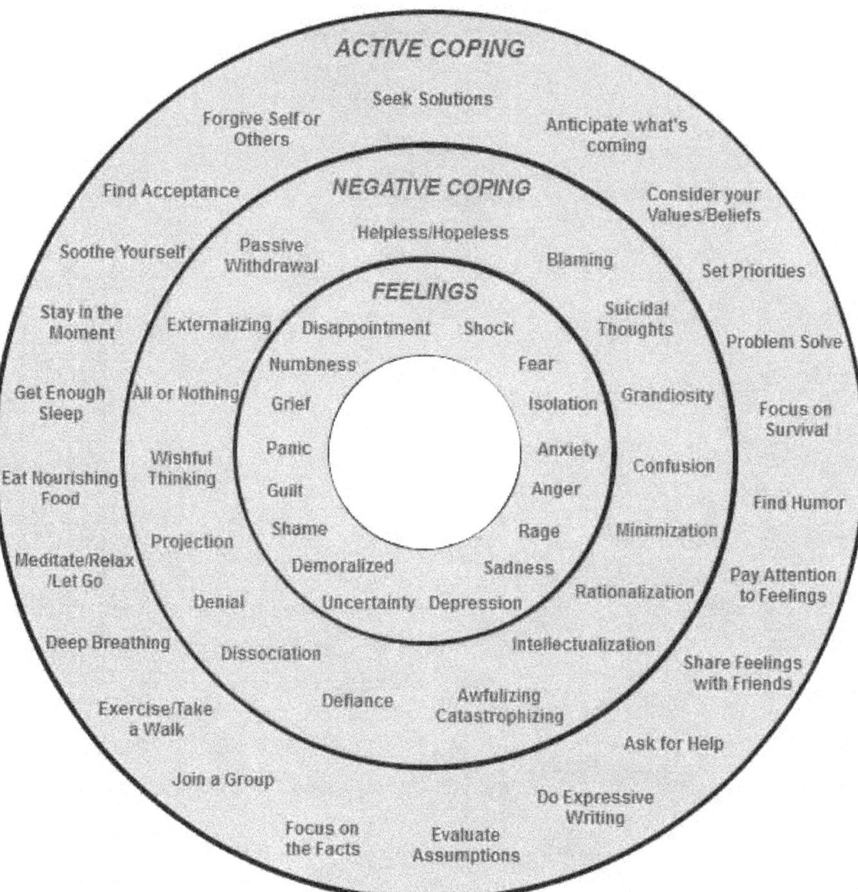

ACTIVE COPING
NEGATIVE COPING
FEELINGS

Seek Solutions
Forgive Self or Others
Anticipate what's coming
Find Acceptance
Consider your Values/Beliefs
Helpless/Hopeless
Blaming
Soothe Yourself
Passive Withdrawal
Set Priorities
Suicidal Thoughts
Stay in the Moment
Externalizing
Disappointment
Shock
Fear
Grandiosity
Problem Solve
Get Enough Sleep
All or Nothing
Grief
Isolation
Focus on Survival
Anxiety
Panic
Wishful Thinking
Confusion
Eat Nourishing Food
Guilt
Anger
Find Humor
Shame
Rage
Minimization
Projection
Demoralized
Sadness
Meditate/Relax /Let Go
Denial
Uncertainty
Depression
Rationalization
Pay Attention to Feelings
Deep Breathing
Dissociation
Intellectualization
Share Feelings with Friends
Defiance
Awfulizing Catastrophizing
Exercise/Take a Walk
Ask for Help
Join a Group
Do Expressive Writing
Focus on the Facts
Evaluate Assumptions

What you are seeing is the inside of an onion, and the another onion when it is not cut. What inner healing ministry means is to simply peal back the layers and get to the root of the problem. What many people in need of inner heal do even particularly Christians is mask their emotions? A psychological term is masking personality.

Masking is a process in which individual changes or "masks" their natural personality to conform to social pressures, abuse, and harassment. An individual may not even know he or she is wearing a mask because it is a behavior that can take many forms.

https://en.wikipedia.org/wiki/Masking_(personality)

Emotions that are usually concealed are anger, anxiety, disgust, embarrassment, fear, frustration and sadness. Masked emotions motions are expressed in place of the concealed emotions: amusement, boredom, contempt, frustration, happiness, interest and sadness.

https://en.wikipedia.org/wiki/Masking_(personality)

Mask are what we hide behind. Christians are infamous for having masks because we are subconsciously taught the only emotion we are supposed to have is happy.

We will talk more about the strategy of inner healing in the chapters to come. The point is when a person is in need of inner healing, we are uncovering the mask; we are peeling back the layers and getting to the cause. After getting to the root, we apply the principles of the word of God, to bring about healing.

A Christ led counselor must be fully equipped, trained, and prepared in all three different aspects of the counseling ministry. We will talk further about this, but as a counselor, you may not be able to go right into inner healing ministry right away because the counselee is very fragile emotionally, so you have to stay at mental health counseling. A person may need deliverance ministry which is the casting out of demons. However, I caution you to use wisdom. You can't counsel a demon you can counsel the person. This is significant because if a person is struggling with unforgiveness, a demon won't come out. I have counseled individuals who the demonic entered them as a result of trauma and chronic fear. That doesn't mean you have to put them out of your office, you still counsel them in love, you teach them the principles of inner healing, and when they are ready you then cast them out.

Many will ask how can a person hear when they are full of demons? It is simple, demons still submit to the blood of Jesus. If you are a spirit led counselor what will happen is the demon or demonic will be silent while you minister inner healing to the person. That doesn't always mean that they are ready to forgive, you give them seeds in time when they are ready for full deliverance they will forgive.

We said you have to be prepared processed into inner healing ministry. Let's back one more time to Isaiah 61 it tells us the qualifications, I know I am being redundant but let us revisit it again.

Isaiah 61:1-2 (TLB)

1 The Spirit of the Lord God is upon me, because the Lord has anointed me to bring good news to the suffering and afflicted. He has sent me to comfort the brokenhearted, to announce liberty to captives, and to open the eyes of the blind.

2 He has sent me to tell those who mourn that the time of God's favor to them has come, and the day of his wrath to their enemies.

The qualifications for inner healing ministry are we must be anointed by the spirit of God. The anointing must not only be upon me, but we must be filled with the Holy Spirit to operate in inner healing. We must also be sent by God to do this kind of work and to minister to those who are broken. Again we must be anointed, appointed, and sent.

One final word of admonishment, it is important to note that all and I do mean all healing work originates from the Bible, which includes mental health counseling, and inner healing. What the secular world does is take these principles and concepts from the Bible and make it their own. What they do is take out the word of God, Jesus, and the Bible, therefore not giving credit to its original owner.

It is important to note that ALL healing work absent from Christ in it, is demonic, yes I said demonic. Just because it appears to be spiritual doesn't mean it is from God. There are many spirits the exist in the world, the Holy Spirit that we operate under is more powerful than any other spirit.

1 John 4:1-3 (KJV)

1 Beloved, believe not every spirit, but try the spirits whether they are of God: because many false prophets are gone out into the world.

2 Hereby know ye the Spirit of God: Every spirit that confesseth that Jesus Christ is come in the flesh is of God:

3 And every spirit that confesseth not that Jesus Christ is come in the flesh is not of God: and this is that spirit of antichrist, whereof ye have heard that it should come; and even now already is it in the world.

This is important to know because there is a big push for inner healing work absent from Christ that the world is enamored by. This television show Iyanla Fix My Life is one of them. I am in no way shape or form, endorsing this television show or shows like it.

The reason I am pointing this out is that throughout the book you will read about different principles that appear to be from the secular word. As a Christian leader and therapist, my commitment is to always lead you the reader to Christ. Every principle is first founded on the word of God, through His son Jesus Christ. I am in no way borrowing from the world, remember they stole from the Bible, not the other way around.

If you see similarities to anything I will always reference scripture, and Jesus to back up my teaching. I want to make a bold public statement that any new age, light work, crystal watching, drawing from other energy sources or healing work absent from Christ is not of God and the work of the imitator satan.

It is thereby understood by you the reader, any word usage, or concepts that you feel maybe similar to something you have seen or heard is not what it looks like everything I will teach you is always from Christ and Christ alone.

I may use words such as healing work, the healing worker, the work of the Holy Spirit, etc. It is understood that these concepts are not nor will they ever been for anything but the blood of Jesus. If I say healing worker, I mean the Holy Spirit led counselor. Every statement I make, every principle I teach is to the glory of the King of Kings and Lord of Lords, Jesus Christ.

Let us continue.

Chapter 2

Where Do We Begin?

Psalm 34:18 (KJV)

18 The Lord is nigh unto them that are of a broken heart; and saveth such as be of a contrite spirit.

Before we get started, it is important to understand the works of the Holy Spirit. We cannot delve into inner healing counseling without the Holy Spirit. Remember I said the number one criteria for being an inner healing counselor is that you must be called, anointed and appointed to the position. You must understand the gifts of the Holy Spirit and His role in the inner healing session.

You must understand the gifts of the spirit, and it's operation. You must understand how to operate in the gifts of the spirit that are already on the inside of you. There has been some confusion in the Christian counseling world whether or not the gifts of the spirit should be used within the counseling session.

This chapter will bring clarity. I am boldly and unapologetically telling you that you cannot implement the true strategies of inner healing without the gifts of the spirit in operation within the counselor. It cannot be done affectively. First, let us delve into what the gifts of the spirit are. Warning I am going to put the same scripture in to different translations to bring further clarity.

1 Corinthians 12:3-10 (KJV)

3 Wherefore I give you to understand, that no man speaking by the Spirit of God calleth Jesus accursed: and that no man can say that Jesus is the Lord, but by the Holy Ghost.

4Now there are diversities of gifts, but the same Spirit.

5 And there are differences of administrations, but the same Lord.

6 And there are diversities of operations, but it is the same God which worketh all in all.

7 But the manifestation of the Spirit is given to every man to profit withal.

8 For to one is given by the Spirit the word of wisdom; to another the word of knowledge by the same Spirit;

9 To another faith by the same Spirit; to another the gifts of healing by the same Spirit;

10 To another the working of miracles; to another prophecy; to another discerning of spirits; to another divers kinds of tongues; to another the interpretation of tongues:

1 Corinthians 12:3-10Living Bible (TLB)

3 But now you are meeting people who claim to speak messages from the Spirit of God. How can you know whether they are really inspired by God or whether they are fakes? Here is the test: no one speaking by the power of the Spirit of God can curse Jesus, and no one can say, "Jesus is Lord," and really mean it, unless the Holy Spirit is helping him.

4 Now God gives us many kinds of special abilities, but it is the same Holy Spirit who is the source of them all.

5 There are different kinds of service to God, but it is the same Lord we are serving.

 6 There are many ways in which God works in our lives, but it is the same God who does the work in and through all of us who are his.

7 The Holy Spirit displays God's power through each of us as a means of helping the entire church.

8 To one person the Spirit gives the ability to give wise advice; someone else may be especially good at studying and teaching, and this is his gift from the same Spirit.

9 He gives special faith to another, and to someone else the power to heal the sick.

10 He gives power for doing miracles to some, and to others power to prophesy and preach. He gives someone else the power to know whether evil spirits are speaking through those who claim to be giving God's messages—or whether it is really the Spirit of God who is speaking. Still another person is able to speak in languages he never learned; and others, who do not know the language either, are given the power to understand what he is saying.

I remember some years ago; I had a friend who struggled with the spirit of fear. I knew this about her without her telling me. The Holy Spirit revealed to me that she had been raped and that is when she started struggling with fear. Now, this happened many years ago, before I was aware of the gifts of the spirit, or how it operates. As a young person, all I knew was that I felt something in my spirit about my friend. One day she says she has something to tell me. She was so afraid to tell me what happened to her; she told me what happened in an email. This was a very long time ago. I am telling my age, but this was before the age of text messages, social media and such. She was so afraid she didn't actually to talk about it. When she told me I wasn't surprised, I just wanted to support my friend and love her unconditionally.

My point is telling you this is that the spirit of God will tell you what is going on with your client long before they will. Sometimes they won't have the words to tell you. Sometimes they will be so fragile they can't talk. Sometimes they will be so traumatized they can't remember what happened to them. We need the Holy Spirit to reveal the truth, and guide the session. My friend was not my client, however, what birthed in me at that time was that I didn't need to hear the person say what happened to them for me to know what happened.

First, let us talk about the gifts of the spirit and how they operate in the inner healing session.

This is not a full teaching on the gifts of the spirit if you want further clarity I encourage you to study more on your own terms about the gifts of the spirit. This chapter is more focused on how the gifts of the Holy Spirit are supposed to be in operation in the counseling session.

It is important to note that the operation of the spirit is not strange, frightening or misleading. I want you to think about how we typically see the gifts of the spirit in operation in the church.

You see someone in a leadership position, being used of God such as a pastor or a prophet. We usually see the demonstration of the Holy Spirit with signs and wonders.

Some great man or woman is in front of an audience; there maybe music playing softly, someone maybe speaking in tongues, there is a big production side of this kind of public ministry. The reason why many Christian led counselors are hesitant to use the gifts of the spirit is because when they think of the gifts in operation, they think of the scenario just mentioned.

In the counseling session, none of this is present. There is no audience; it's just you and the counselee. There is no music. I am a tongue talking Christian. In my practice I meet with many people, many are unbelieving, I don't typically speak in tongues in front of them because I don't want to scare them. Just because you are not making it a big show doesn't mean that the gifts of the spirit are not operating. Just because you are in a session with an unbeliever doesn't mean your Holy Spirit administered gifts shut off.

You just have to use wisdom. I am not saying don't speak in tongues in front of your client. I am again saying use wisdom. You have to know and discern who is in front of you. Often I meet with people who are not Christian, or if they are they don't understand the gifts of the spirit. If I start off speaking in tongues suddenly with no explanation, they will be scared and probably never return.

I was discussing with a cousin of my a few weeks ago. She is an older woman, who attends church but is not familiar with the moves of God. She told us how she was confused after interacting with a friend, who prayed with her began to speak in tongues, but she didn't understand what was going on because she wasn't familiar with moves of God. I am not saying the person who prayed with her was wrong; I am saying use wisdom. My cousin left the prayer confused because there was no explanation of what was going on or why. It is not that she was rebellious or not open to the moves of God she just wasn't familiar with it and because there was no explanation she still went away from the prayer confused. As she discussed with me and my family we talked to her more about it and it made better sense to her.

Execution of the gifts of the spirit within the counseling session must be done delicately because the person in front of you is very fragile. Delivery should be done as if one is having a conversation. Your client may not know that you are operating in the gifts of the spirit. Remember we are to lead people to the cross of Jesus, we don't always give them the answers right away.

One of my professors in college told us that there is a right way and a wrong way to help people. We help them the wrong way when we help them in such a way that they become dependent upon us. We help them the right way when they become self-sufficient. Now my professor was not a Christian counselor, but I caught that in the spirit.

We can give the counselee the answers in such a way, that they become dependent on us. However, that is the wrong way to help people. When ministering healing to the counselee we must do it in such a way that it leads them to the cross of Jesus, then we have helped them in the most appropriate right way. Remember we are servant leaders, we lead people to Christ, we serve others, we are not to seek our own glory.

When we use the gifts of the spirit to bring any form of glory or adoration to us, we then become guilty of operating under a wrong spirit. The gifts of the spirit always lead people to Jesus Christ, not us, or another man.

I am going to highlight some of the main functions of the Holy Spirit that we should use to minister healing to the counselee. Remember that the Holy Spirit will not come in unless He is first invited. Have you invited the Holy Spirit into your practice? Do you recognize Him as the ultimate counselor? We are simple servant leaders it is the Holy Spirit who does the work. As counselor's the more we recognize our absolute dependence on the Holy Spirit the better things will be.

You can always pray that the Lord would lead the session. Sometimes you won't always know what to say or even how to say it. However, the Holy Spirit knows and sees. He understands, He is the best counselor there is, again the more we rely on Him, we ensure that the counselee will be made whole. We are not the healers; we lead them to the healer. He does the work it is our responsibility to allow Him to lead.

Ask yourself the question do you have a relationship with the Holy Spirit. Again there are many great counselors out there, but without the Holy Spirit, we are nothing. If you don't allow Him to lead He won't. This is where Christian counseling is very different from secular counseling. They see the same clients for the same reason for 5, 10 and 15 years for the same issue. Sometimes they see client's for a lifetime? Why because it is the work of the Holy Spirit to heal, the secular world counsels people without the Holy Spirit. Only lasting and permanent healing happens when the Holy Spirit is present.

We won't be able to talk about all the functions of the Holy Spirit but again I will highlight some of the main functions of the gift as we operate in the session. Some of the main functions that we will talk about is that the Holy Spirit is a counselor, comforter, revealer of truth, within that comes words of knowledge, words of wisdom, the prophetic.

First let us talk about the obvious, the Holy Spirit as a counselor. I don't know about you but in graduate school we learned all about different theoretical approaches to work with client's. We learned what to say, how to say, what not to say. For example as a therapist we are warned not to self-disclose, we learn boundaries with clients. We learn how to deal with client's who are suicidal, to be honest many years ago, when I was about to graduate it felt overwhelming. In fact one of my classmates said a few days before we were to graduate how she was worried that she didn't have enough information or wasn't ready to work with clients. I secretly felt the same way. Years of study, late nights, paperwork, internships, and we all felt inadequate. I realized many years later that it is impossible to know everything you are supposed to know before you begin meeting with clients.

Imagine I finally got the job of my dreams. I am scheduled for a full day. Eight different client's that day, with eight different issues. Of course, some of them have similar issues, some of them the same mental health diagnosis, but they are still individually different, some children, some adults, and others I had to meet with the families. For some issues, I never studied in the textbooks, or we briefly skimmed the subject. Does that mean I am an inadequate therapist? No, it means I am human.

Believe it or not, this relates to using inner healing. Times like these I am glad I am a Christian first. As a Christian therapist, you must have a relationship with not only God but the Holy Spirit. There are many different reasons to be aligned with the Holy Spirit. However for the sake of this book, we will talk about how He is the counselor, we are simply the servant by which He will speak through.

Humor me for a minute I know we all know what a counselor is but for the sake of the text let's go there. A counselor is a person trained to give guidance on personal, social, or psychological problems. A person who gives advice on a specified subject.

Yet what do you do when you're like me faced with so many complex issues in one day? Imagine in a full week. My resolve and what should be yours is you must lean on the Holy Spirit.

Often I talk to Holy Spirit and say, "Holy Spirit I am not the real counselor you are, I need you to counsel these people, not me." He will speak through me.

Look what God says about the Holy Spirit,

Mark 13:11 (NKJV)

11 But when they arrest you and deliver you up, do not worry beforehand, or premeditate[a] what you will speak. But whatever is given you in that hour, speak that; for it is not you who speak, but the Holy Spirit

Beforehand means an action or event; in advance. Premediate think out or plan (an action) beforehand. I am not suggesting that my study or preparation was in vain. I am not suggesting that you don't prepare to be a counselor. I am saying with it is the Holy Spirit that we lean on Him to counsel not ourselves. We may never know everything that we are supposed to know and say, but the Holy Spirit does. You still have to study and prepare. Holy Spirit will not bring back to your memory what you have not prepared for.

John 14:26 (NKJV)

26 But the Helper, the Holy Spirit, whom the Father will send in My name, He will teach you all things, and bring to your remembrance all things that I said to you.

Notice it says that He will teach you all things. I cannot tell you how many times the Lord has had me study on a certain topic then I am already well versed in what they are going through because God had me studying and preparing beforehand for a client I didn't even know I would meet. That is no coincident. Often when I study I don't know why I am studying a particular topic or intervention, but God does. In session, Holy Spirit brings it back to your memory.

Let us look at what else the Holy Spirit does.

John 16:13 (NKJV)

13 However, when He, the Spirit of truth, has come, He will guide you into all truth; for He will not speak on His own authority, but whatever He hears He will speak; and He will tell you things to come.

Look at the scripture is describes the Holy Spirit as the Spirit of truth. He cannot lie. Imagine with me how this works in session. Say you have a client's who presents with all kinds of issues related to chronic anxiety, otherwise known as fear. When you ask them what may have triggered this, they say, "I don't know all the sudden one day it happened out of the clear blue.".

This is where the gifts of the Spirit come in. The Holy Spirit will tell you what the person experienced. We know this as the word of knowledge. Meaning the Holy Spirit reveals the hidden things in that person that they may not know or they may not want to reveal. I meet with client's all the time who experience sexual abuse. Some may not want to let me know what happened or how it happened. If it is relevant to the person's healing Holy Spirit will reveal what you need to know. By the way, nothing just happens.

The word of knowledge is often defined as the ability of one person to know what God is currently doing or intends to do in the life of another person. It can also be defined as knowing the secrets of another's person's heart. Word of knowledge is also meant to reveal hidden secrets from the past.

It was a known fact that God would reveal to the prophet Elisha what the king's plan was in secret.

2 Kings 6:12Living Bible (TLB)

12 "It's not us, sir," one of the officers replied. "Elisha, the prophet, tells the king of Israel even the words you speak in the privacy of your bedroom!"

That wasn't some special gift in Elisha that was the Holy Spirit, revealing secrets.

Notice according to John 16 the Holy Spirit is a guide. That means in session the Holy Spirit guides the session. He dictates the way in which we should go within the counseling session.

Hopefully, you can see how being a spirit led Christian counselor is very different from the secular therapist. Secular therapist lean on their own understanding and secular interventions, they don't have the supernatural knowledge and ability from the Holy Spirit that we have. You can't utilize the benefits of the Holy Spirit without being a Christian and having a relationship with the Holy Spirit. This is important because just because someone is a Christian doesn't mean they have a relationship with the Holy Spirit. If you are going to do affective inner healing work you have to understand how a relationship with the Holy Spirit works, and how to operate in the gifts of the Holy Spirit.

The other thing that we must know about the gifts of the spirit is the word of wisdom, prophetic gifting and how they operate within the inner healing session. Simply a word of wisdom is supernatural knowledge about what direction to take. There are many examples as found in the word of God. One example that comes to mind is Joseph who interprets a dream for the Pharaoh. By the way dream interpretation is a gift of the spirit. It falls under the word of knowledge category. Genesis 41. After Joseph interprets the dream, he then gives the Pharaoh clear instructions as to how to move forward.

This is something to keep in mind because often you will meet with client's who have very vivid dreams. It is like God is trying to get a message to them, but they more than likely will not understand, this is where your relationship with the Holy Spirit comes in.

This is the pattern of the counseling session; you may be given a word of knowledge from the Holy Spirit regarding your client. It may come as a dream they had, but not always. When you are spirit led the Holy

Spirit will give you clear instructions as to what the counselee should do. In the mental health world, we call it therapeutic homework. Therapeutic homework can be written or verbal. The other day I told my client to look up as many scriptures as she can on fear and bring them back to our next session.

Then there is the prophetic anointing. There is no way I will be able to even tap into how the prophetic anointing operates. I must tell you that the prophetic anointing does work within the counseling session. I have prophesied that my clients would find jobs, homes, you name it. True prophecy is not always flesh pleasing either. Prophecy can come as a warning. Unfortunately, I had a client that I was trying to refer to substance abuse treatment. He repeatedly declined my referral. There was nothing I could do after countless times of me telling him he needed to go, after finding the place he could go and making sure he had an appointment. Unfortunately, he died of a drug overdose.

It does happen, that someone needs more than we can give. Or they need another level of care before they can do inner healing work. I gave you an example because I warned him but he didn't listen. Eventually he dropped off my radar because he wasn't following up with me either, it is sad when young people die

My point is the prophetic anointing works within the counseling session. Again you have to use wisdom. You can't look at what you see in church as your model. I am not against speaking in tongues, playing music, setting the atmosphere, and doing the performance. I am for having a conversation with my clients. Remember the word of knowledge has more to do with revealing the secrets or the past, the prophetic anointing as to do with future.

Ironically when someone is stuck in depression, their thoughts focus on the past. When someone is stuck in anxiety, they are worried about the future. We simply have to change emotional lanes and allow the power of God to undercover hidden motives, to bring healing. Then we encourage with the prophetic to bring hope.

Beloved there is so much more I can say about how the Holy Spirit operates within the session. The gifts of the spirit are inside of you. If you are not familiar with the gifts of the spirit, I encourage you to begin your own study.

My hope is at least I answered the question that the gifts of the spirit should ALWAYS be used within the context of the inner healing Christian counselor.

Chapter 3

What Are Inner Vows?

Ecclesiastes 5:4-6 (KJV)

4 When thou vowest a vow unto God, defer not to pay it; for he hath no pleasure in fools: pay that which thou hast vowed.

5 Better is it that thou shouldest not vow, than that thou shouldest vow and not pay.

6 Suffer not thy mouth to cause thy flesh to sin; neither say thou before the angel, that it was an error: wherefore should God be angry at thy voice, and destroy the work of thine hands?

When working with the counselees, you must determine what their inner vow is. It will make sense as we go through this chapter. A vow is a solemn promise, oath, pledge, promise, bond, covenant, commitment, avowal, profession, affirmation, attestation, assurance, guarantee.

First, let's start by talking about the power of the vow and how it is so important to explore within the inner healing counseling session. Let us look at a few scriptures before we go into the meat of the text.

Proverbs 18:21 (KJV)

21 Death and life are in the power of the tongue: and they that love it shall eat the fruit thereof.

It is very important that we don't make a vow before God. Let's go back to the original scripture we read in Ecclesiastes, believe me, it is going to make total sense read on.

What we speak we have the ability to make come to fruition. Most of us think of this as a positive, and it is, trust me it is. God gives us a lot of power and authority.

Matthew 18:18 (NKJV)

18 "Assuredly, I say to you, whatever you bind on earth will be bound in heaven, and whatever you loose on earth will be loosed in heaven.

God intends for us to be free, operate in power and authority. We have a lot of power that lies within our tongue.

James 3:2-4Living Bible (TLB)

If anyone can control his tongue, it proves that he has perfect control over himself in every other way.

3 We can make a large horse turn around and go wherever we want by means of a small bit in his mouth.

4 And a tiny rudder makes a huge ship turn wherever the pilot wants it to go, even though the winds are strong.So there is power in the mouth. How does this relate to inner vows? I am glad you asked.

Imagine with me you have a client, who comes in your office. They suffer from chronic relationship problems. You prayed with them, counseled them on healthy versus unhealthy relationships but still, the individual keeps experiencing chronic issues. They keep having problems with different family members, friends, and potential mates. The common denominator is them. However no matter the counseling technique you have to get them to understand inner vows.

So you pray asking Holy Spirit to reveal what you are not seeing. He responds, "inner vows."

What in the world does that mean?

Here is the answer.

As you seek further clarification, you must go back to the root. The counselee experienced severe trauma as a child. As a result of that trauma, they made an inner vow. "No one will ever disrespect me again; I will never allow anyone to hurt me again. I will never marry a man like my father; I will never be like my mother." That my friends is an inner vow.

So how does that impact them? Unconsciously after making the inner vow, a supernatural spirit or force comes upon them. They stay in constant conflict with themselves and other people because of the inner vow they made.

What happens when a person makes an inner is that something happened a life event, a divorce, a traumatic experience, a troubled childhood. Then that person subconsciously or even consciously makes inner vows. Inner vows always have words like (never, always, forever) something permanent. What happens is the supernatural force field begins to create a world that we have spoken into existence. This inner vow creates what we call a word curse.

A word curse is a solemn utterance intended to invoke a supernatural power to inflict harm or punishment on someone or something. The unfortunate things are that a word curse most often affects us more than they affect other people.

I want to warn you I am not suggesting that we have no balance. There is nothing wrong with setting standards of how we want to be treated, particularly when you know what it is like to be mistreated. It becomes not balanced when it is unhealthy.

The reality is even good people offend you unconsciously. No one is perfect, if you make an inner vow with no forgiveness or without the love of Christ, what we think is meant for our protection is meant for our demise.

So as a counselor again you look at the onset or root? You ask the counselee about their childhood, what was it like? Was there any abuse or neglect? What were their parents like? If there was any abuse, trauma, neglect or mistreatment, you have to search further and ask if they made any inner vows.

Other things we must consider are generational curses. Let me give you an example. Many years I was struggling with a particular issue. I remember praying, fasting, reading my word but I couldn't get free from the spirit of fear. I remember praying one day about it, and the Lord gave me a word of knowledge about a relative four generations above me who had made an inner vow which had an impact on me generations later.

Deuteronomy 5:10

…… I will bring the curse of a father's sins upon even the third and fourth generation of the children of those who hate me;…..

You see when God releases a curse it is to the 3rd and 4th generation. My point is a counselee may have never made an inner vow themselves that doesn't mean an inner vow is not present. This is why you need the help of the Holy Spirit, an individual more than likely won't know anything about an inner vows generations above them. What if you are working with an individual who was adopted and has no contact with their family of origin? If you are working with someone who does you can simply ask about patterns they see within their generational line.

If they are adopted and have no clue, you can still pray against inner vows that are in the generational line; you just can't be as specific as you would if you knew the family of origins pattern. Real deliverance can still take place.

Iyanla Vanzant borrowed this right out of scripture; she calls it patterns and pathologies. In her own words;

"We all have patterns of thought, belief, and behavior that we inherit from our family of origin. In the same way that our ears, our eyes, our nose, and the texture of our hair are inherited, we inherit certain mental, emotional, and even spiritual proclivities. We call them habits. Habits are hard to break and, despite our most earnest efforts, we usually remain loyal to our family patterns, even when they are dysfunctional. It is a function of the family cloth from which we are cut."

https://www.healyourlife.com/the-fabric-of-your-being

As stated this is another biblical concept that the world system has borrowed from its origin the bible, and renamed it something else.

So how do we fix it?

Again the Holy Spirit to be our guide, once your ear is in tune to His voice, He reveals what the inner vow was. As you the counselor becomes aware you don't just go and tell the client's what you hear from God unless you are led to do so. Remember counseling is about leading them to the water, it is not about answering the questions straight away. You have to lead the counselee to their own insight.

This happened with Jesus. A father brought his son to Jesus to be healed look at how Jesus responds. He asked a question he already had the answer to.

How do we know He already knew the answer, because He was still God in the flesh, and God knows all things.

Mark 9:17-22 (NLT)

17 One of the men in the crowd spoke up and said, "Teacher, I brought my son so you could heal him. He is possessed by an evil spirit that won't let him talk.

18 And whenever this spirit seizes him, it throws him violently to the ground. Then he foams at the mouth and grinds his teeth and becomes rigid.[a] So I asked your disciples to cast out the evil spirit, but they couldn't do it."

19 Jesus said to them,[b] "You faithless people! How long must I be with you? How long must I put up with you? Bring the boy to me."

20 So they brought the boy. But when the evil spirit saw Jesus, it threw the child into a violent convulsion, and he fell to the ground, writhing and foaming at the mouth.

21 **"How long has this been happening?"** Jesus asked the boy's father.

He replied, "Since he was a little boy.

22 The spirit often throws him into the fire or into water, trying to kill him. Have mercy on us and help us, if you can."

The story was more about the father's unbelief rather than Jesus ability to heal the boy. Notice Jesus asked the father how long this had been happening?

Two questions the counselor must ask, when did this first happen? How long has it been happening? If whatever is going on with them is a onetime event, there may not be a generational curse or inner vow involved. If it happened from a child, and has been ongoing for years then it maybe an inner vow and generational curse.

The counselee must be able to talk about it. After that then you can assist them to point out the inner vow that they made.

They must ask for forgiveness for the inner vow. I didn't say they have to ask for forgiveness for what happened to them. You can't be held responsible for what abuse you suffered. Forgiveness simply means to release the hold that the event has on us. For those caught up in a generational curse they still have to act on behave of their relatives generations above them. The counselee must forgive the offense and ask for forgiveness for the inner vow made as a result of the offense.

Then after they repent, and forgive they must pray a renouncing praying. The renouncing prayer releases the grip of the enemy from using that inner vow against them. Renounce means declare that one will no longer engage in or support. Renounce also means refuse to recognize or abide by any longer.

You then want to allow the Holy Spirit through a prayer to fill the space that the inner vow once had a grip on. Never leave a spot that was once filled by a negative evil spirit or emotion empty.

You still have to contract for follow up counseling sessions, because you now have to counsel the person on how to go through life without their old coping mechanisms. Say they renounced an inner vow that caused unhealthy relationships; you still have to counsel and teach on how to go about and interact in healthy relationships.

When things become habits and ways of life that have existed for generations it becomes hard to break. So you the counselor have to introduce new healthy habits and ways of coping, that can't be done in one single session. After you give the counselee new information, you give them time to implement in their every day life, that includes following up with them in the next sessions.

Remember inner healing is about pealing back the layers, removing unhealthy spirits, unhealthy coping, bringing them to the surface, deliverance happens and the introducing them to a new way of life.

Again never remove the old without introducing the new. Don't be the preacher who only preaches about sin without introducing the joys of salvation.

Isaiah 43:19 (NKJV)

19 Behold, I will do a new thing,

Now it shall spring forth;

Shall you not know it?

I will even make a road in the wilderness

And rivers in the desert.

The old and the new most work together.

Let us continue to our next chapter the root of bitterness.

Chapter 4

The Root Of Bitterness

Hebrews 12:15 (KJV)

15 Looking diligently lest any man fail of the grace of God; lest any root of bitterness springing up trouble you, and thereby many be defiled;

Bitterness is a deadly poison that can destroy your mind, your body and your soul. When working with an individual, you must assess for where the root of bitterness is. There are those who will tell you that there is no root of bitterness. We talked about in previous chapters how we use the gifts of the spirit in the counseling session to allow the Holy Spirit to reveal truth. Just like inner vows can be hidden, so can the root of bitterness. This chapter gets very interesting let us study on together.

First what is the root of bitterness?

Bitterness is anger and disappointment about being mistreated, unfairly or resentment. Resentment is a feeling of indignant displeasure or persistent ill will at something regarded as a wrong, insult, or injury. Indignation anger or annoyance provoked by what is perceived as unfair treatment. All the words defined sum up to one thing bitterness. Believe it or not, bitterness is a negative seed that is sown in us. If we don't remove the seed, it will grow into something large that we cannot control.

Before we move forward, we must also look at the fruit of bitterness. Remember I said bitterness is a seed that grows like a tree. It starts a seed, then if allowed or is not uprooted, it becomes a tree. A fruit barring tree. The fruit that bitterness brings is a poison apple, it will only destroy.

Other fruits of bitterness include; anger, intense rage, and anger. The bible doesn't tell us that we are never to get angry, it tells us don't allow anger to lead to sin. There is a kind of anger that we call helpful anger. Go with me okay. Examples of helpful anger could be someone in an abusive relationship; they get so fed up they leave because they are sick and tired. Martin Luther King started a movement against racial injustice or prejudice because he was tired of the treatment of minorities. The organization MADD was established in the 80's after a mother's 13 year old daughter was killed by a drunk driver. The organization thrives today; the organizers were tired of burying their children due to drunk drivers.

My point is if your anger leads you to change for the positive or changes the world in a positive way, it is not bitterness or anger that becomes sin. However, anger in the wrong direction can lead to sin.

Ephesians 4:26 (KJV)

26 Be ye angry, and sin not: let not the sun go down upon your wrath:

Ephesians 4:31 (KJV)

31 Let all bitterness, and wrath, and anger, and clamour, and evil speaking, be put away from you, with all malice:

If you look at the two scriptures found in Ephesians, one scripture says "be angry", the other scripture says, "put away anger."

If one is not spiritual, it will appear as if the scripture is contradicting itself. I promise you it does not. Anger unchecked leads to sin. Wrath simply means extreme anger. It works like this something makes us angry, instead of checking it, we fester on it, we allow what happened to replay over and over again in our heads, we begin to ruminate on what happened, the next thing you know anger turns into wrath, which is extreme anger. Devastating things begin to happen when wrath is present. I know I am giving you a lot of information, but I promise it relates to inner healing, you want to be able to minister true emotional healing to those you serve. We can't bypass roots of bitterness to get there. Let us look at a powerful example as found in the word of God.

Genesis 4:1-8Living Bible (TLB)

4 Then Adam had sexual intercourse with Eve his wife, and she conceived and gave birth to a son, Cain (meaning "I have created"). For, as she said, "With God's help, I have created a man!"

 2 Her next child was his brother, Abel.

Abel became a shepherd, while Cain was a farmer.

 3 At harvest time Cain brought the Lord a gift of his farm produce,

4 and Abel brought the fatty cuts of meat from his best lambs, and presented them to the Lord. And the Lord accepted Abel's offering,

5 but not Cain's. This made Cain both dejected and very angry, and his face grew dark with fury.

6 "Why are you angry?" the Lord asked him. "Why is your face so dark with rage?

 7 It can be bright with joy if you will do what you should! But if you refuse to obey, watch out. Sin is waiting to attack you, longing to destroy you. But you can conquer it!"

8 One day Cain suggested to his brother, "Let's go out into the fields." And while they were together there, Cain attacked and killed his brother.

Most of us should know the story of Cain and Abel by now. Within the text we read I want to point out the relationship between Cain and God. God didn't love Abel more than he loved Cain. Abel simply offered up what was an appropriate sacrifice, while Cain had not. If you have more than one child you know they don't all do the right things at the same time. Sometimes you correct one, other times you correct the other one. This was simply Cain's time of correction. I am sure Abel had his life not been cut short would have had a time of correction before God, because he wasn't perfect, he was a human just like the rest of us.

Cain became angry at God. It doesn't say Cain was angry at Abel; it didn't say they argued. Scripture doesn't say Cain and Abel were close; it doesn't say they were not close. I believe Cain was envious of Abel. Envy means a feeling of discontented or resentful longing aroused by someone else's possessions, qualities, or luck. Cain was angry at God. God as a loving Father knew what was in Cain's heart and He warned him. Let us look at verse 7 in a different text.

Genesis 4:7 (NKJV)

7 If you do well, will you not be accepted? And if you do not do well, sin lies at the door. And its desire is for you, but you should rule over it."

I hope you are catching this. Sin when unchecked, has a desire. The text says that it lies at the door of our hearts, it has a desire to control us. Cain never checked the root of bitterness he had, in the following text he killed his brother.

When we continue in a root of bitterness, it will consume our very being. It leads to death. Death of our will, our mind, our emotions. Bitterness becomes a debilitating disease, that desires to take full control of us.

In fact, social scientist are becoming more and more privy to how bitterness works, they propose that bitterness can even lead to a severe mental illness.

Posttraumatic embitterment disorder (PTED) is a proposed disorder modeled after posttraumatic stress disorder. Some psychiatrists are proposing this as a mental disorder because they believe that there are people who have become so bitter, they can barely function.[1] PTED patients do not fit the formal criteria for PTSD and can be clinically distinguished from it, prompting the description of a new and separate disorder.[2][3]

https://en.wikipedia.org/wiki/Posttraumatic_embitter ment_disorder

German psychiatrist Michael Linden, who has conducted research on the proposed disorder,[4] describes its effect on people: "They feel the world has treated them unfairly. It's one step more complex than anger. They're angry plus helpless." He says that people with the disorder are almost treatment resistant and that; "These people usually don't come to treatment because 'the world has to change, not me.'" He believes that 1 to 2 percent of people are affected at any given time, and explains that, although sufferers of the disorder tend to have a desire for vengeance, "...Revenge is not a treatment."[3]

https://en.wikipedia.org/wiki/Posttraumatic_embitterment_disorder

Again because it is a proposed disorder it has not made it into the DSM as of yet. For those who are not aware the DSM-IV is what we licensed therapist to use as a diagnostic tool for assessing for a mental illness.

My point is to notice how it says they become so bitter they can hardly function. Remember where there is no emotional or mental change in the disposition of the counselee, there is always a root of bitterness present.

You cannot receive grace nor can you forgive or give grace where bitterness is present. Bitterness clouds your judgement and makes you see everything from a negative point of view.

Hebrews 12:15 (NKJV)

15 looking carefully lest anyone fall short of the grace of God; lest any root of bitterness springing up cause trouble, and by this many become defiled;

Notice the scripture says bitterness defiles you. Defile means to make impure and unclean. Defile also means to contaminate, taint, pollute, contaminate implies intrusion of or contact with dirt or foulness from an outside source.

When you are filled with bitterness, no one wants to around you because even if you don't say anything you contaminate the atmosphere. People filled with the root of bitterness are very unhappy, unhealthy people. Bitterness is like cancer it will spread.

How to minister healing to the counselee who has a root of bitterness;

I want to warn you this is very difficult because someone who has a root of bitterness, will think everyone is wrong but them. They are very defensive, and it is hard to present truth to them.

Let's Review:

First as stated operate in the gifts of the spirit, focusing on the word of knowledge.

This is important because when a person has root of bitterness, they more than likely won't recognize it has such.

You have teach the counselee how the root of bitterness works. You also have to teach them about how forgiveness works. Focusing on this particular topic will more than likely take more than one session.

You ask them based upon the information that was discussed do they see any area where there is a root of bitterness in them? Yes Holy Spirit may have revealed it to you but the point is to lead them to come to their own insight about the matter

If they say yes or no, still point out where the Holy Spirit has revealed where the root of bitterness is.

The counselor points this out in a non-judgmental way. Use suggestive reasoning as a technique to counsel. Suggestive reasoning simply is when you ask certain questions in a way to get the counselee to think.

Ask them what does it cost them to keep holding on to the offense? (ie responses could be not happy, not being able to enjoy life, being stuck in the past.)

By the way I am not suggesting that an offense didn't take place, when a person is stuck in the root of bitterness something that happened in the past, is consuming their lives as if it happened yesterday, it could be an offense that happened 10 or 15 years ago.

Then you ask them what would they have to give up? If a person gives up bitterness they would have to give up feeling sorry for themselves, excuses, etc.

In the counseling word we call this secondary gains. It means when a counselee gains some unhealthy advantage to remaining sick. Examples could be they elicit attention, people feel sorry for them, etc.

If they are still willing to go through the healing process you lead them to a prayer of forgiveness, and repentance. They forgive whoever has offended them. They still have to repent for allowing the root of bitterness to take root and impact their life in such a powerful. You can't always help what happened to you, you can help your response.

You still have to contract for more counseling sessions, again this shouldn't be done in one session. After the person receives healing you still again have to remove old habits that were rooted in bitterness, and introduce new habits. You have to teach them how to allow the fruit of the spirit to reign. Offenses will come after a person has been delivered, but again if they know a new way to respond the root of bitterness won't return with a vengeance. If you leave them with no tools the root of bitterness will return with a vengeance. Next we must talk about how forgiveness is healing. An individual will never experience emotional healing and wholeness without forgiveness.

A fair warning, I have written an entire book entitled: *Healing The Heart Through Forgiveness.*

Instead of writing an entire new chapter I am going to simply add one chapter from that book. I encourage you to pick up the the book; there is great revelation when we learn the power of forgiveness. You may want to recommend it to some of your counselee's. Particularly the ones who are stuck in the root of bitterness.

Chapter 5

How Forgiveness Heals

Luke 23:34 (KJV)

34 Then said Jesus, Father, forgive them; for they know not what they do. And they parted his raiment, and cast lots.

Immaculee IIibagiza survived the Rwandan Genocide. In 1994 there was political unrest and ongoing tensions between two tribes the Hutu and Tutsi. The tension led to the murders of thousands of the Tutsi tribe. Immaculee's family was one of the many who became victim to these crimes against humanity. Immaculee's entire family was murdered while she and seven other women hid in a small bathroom for three months. Immaculee went on to write a New York Times bestselling book entitled, Left To Tell and Led By Faith.

Eventually Immaculee did meet one of the murderers face to face where she told him that she forgave him.

Forgiveness is defined as to cease with resentment, bitterness or anger towards someone that has caused a great offense. It means to grant a pardon. It means to let go of. It means to not hold oneself or another hostage over the offense or offenses.

Remember what we studied about the root of bitterness in the previous chapter. Freedom from the stronghold of bitterness cannot happen without forgiveness.

Forgiveness also means to release and to pardon, towards another. It means to not carry the wrongful acts, done to us in our yesterday into our today, to impact our tomorrow. Forgiveness is the emotional and spiritual act of wiping away the hurt, pain, and turmoil.

Forgiveness is the conscious act, and deliberate decision to release feelings of resentment or vengeance towards a person or group who has harmed you, regardless of whether or not they deserve your forgiveness.

Forgiveness is not earned, it is granted. Forgiveness is a decision. Forgiveness cannot be forced upon you. Forgiveness can be a hard concept for any individuals to conceive of. Most people can't really conceive of why you would forgive someone who has hurt you particularly with some of the tragic things that are recently going on in our nation.

Forgiveness is the divine order of God. The only way we have access to the kingdom of God next to salvation and sanctification is forgiveness.

The reality is whatever the offender has done, holding it in your heart, mind, and spirit will not help the situation. It will not make what happened go away. It does not hurt the offender. In fact, in some ways it empowers them. For some the offender knew the intended damage it would have on you, and it still has power over you, their intentions were malicious. When you continue to hold on to it, you are giving them the power in your heart.

You can have unforgiveness in your heart towards a dead person. Unforgiveness impacts the mind, the will, and the emotions. Unforgiveness creates a broken, damaged and emotionally wounded heart. The reality is there is no recompense in unforgiveness. Recompense is compensation or reward given for loss or harm suffered or effort made. You can't reap the reward of wholeness and a healed heart when you don't forgive.

First, let us begin by looking at what scripture has to say about forgiveness.

Romans 5:8 (NKJV)

8 But God demonstrates His own love toward us, in that while we were still sinners, Christ died for us.

1 John 1:9 (NKJV)

9 If we confess our sins, He is faithful and just to forgive us our sins and to cleanse us from all unrighteousness.

John 3:16 (KJV)

16 For God so loved the world, that he gave his only begotten Son, that whosoever believeth in him should not perish, but have everlasting life.

The first thing about forgiveness is that it originated from God Himself. Man did not come up with the idea or principle of forgiveness that is why it is so hard for people who are not Christians to understand the concept of forgiveness. The kingdom of God is all about love. Therefore strife, division, dissention, ill will, hurt, bitterness, anxiety, death, and destruction do not exist in the kingdom of God. These things came to exist as a result of the first rebellion in heaven and the sin that Adam and Eve committed in the garden.

Man was introduced to these concepts that never existed prior. God never had to ask anyone for forgiveness, because He never did anything wrong. Satan is the one who rebelled and committed the first sin, not Adam and Eve as some imply.

The devil was the worship leader in heaven. He decided he didn't want to be the worship leader he wanted to be worshipped. Even in heaven, the only being that was ever worshiped was God. Satan decided that He wanted to be God. Many people imply that satan wanted to be like God, no that is not true. Satan wanted to be God Himself. If your heart is truly for the Lord, you want to be like Him. That was not satan's motive. He wanted admiration, and worship. He desired power, prominence and position so he pursued it by any means necessary. There was a big revolt in heaven and the devil deceived many of the angels. He was evicted from heaven, and his angels. Now he still wants to be God, however he will

never. My point is satan committed the first sin.
However to date he has never asked for forgiveness,
never repented and he has never admitted that he was
wrong.

However after satan did what he did, sin entered into
existence. It was Adam and Eve who introduced sin to
earth. Now we are all born into sin.

So everyone is in need of the savior Jesus, and we
need to confess our sin, in order to be forgiven.

Psalm 51:5 (KJV)

5 Behold, I was shapen in iniquity; and in sin did my
mother conccive me.

Because sin is in us, everyone at some point in their
lives has committed a sin, most of us many sins.

Romans 3:22-23 (NKJV)

22 even the righteousness of God, through faith in
Jesus Christ, to all and on all[a] who believe. For
there is no difference; 23 for all have sinned and
fallen short of the glory of God

We all have a sin conscious. It means to be aware, to
be pulled, lured or enticed by a sin or wrong doing.
Sin simply means to act, think, practice or display

behaviors that are contrary to the word of God. It means to act unrighteous, and to do wrong.

We read Romans 5:8 that says Christ died for us when we were still sinners. Meaning Christ made the ultimate sacrifice which was death to atone for our sin. Atone means to make amends. Before we thought to ask for forgiveness, He went ahead and died. We hadn't asked for forgiveness, felt sorry for what we had done, or thought that we did anything wrong He died.

He didn't just die for Christians, He died for the entire world. Meaning Christ decided to forgive us of what did before we did it. He decided to forgive us before we asked it. Now that is the powerful thing about forgiveness. Even now you can forgive someone without them ever acknowledging that they offended you.

We forgive because we are forgiven.

Ephesians 4:32 (NKJV)

32 And be kind to one another, tenderhearted, forgiving one another, even as God in Christ forgave you

When you claim to be a Christian you are making the proclamation that you have been forgiven by Christ. You have confessed Him as Lord and savior. We all have had incidents where we have had to ask for forgiveness to one another. The reality is we error in one way or the other, whether it be intentional or unintentional. Sometimes you can have the right motives but go about it the wrong way. Sometimes you were just wrong and had to humble yourself admit it and move forward. Think about a time you offended someone. Clearly you had to go back to that person and ask to be forgiven. We all have, that is a part of human nature.

The reality is if you don't forgive others, God won't forgive you.

Matthew 6:14-15 (NKJV)

14 "For if you forgive men their trespasses, your heavenly Father will also forgive you. 15 But if you do not forgive men their trespasses, neither will your Father forgive your trespasses

Remember I said that in the kingdom of heaven things like bitterness, envy, hatred, unforgiveness don't exist. The only way to enter the kingdom is to repent of your sins and ask Christ into your heart. You can't gain access to this kingdom with these things in your heart. The kingdom is the most powerful entity that exists. To be able to seek, obtain entrance to this kingdom, you need to first meet the requirements. Since the first requirement is repentance, if you don't meet the requirements you don't gain access. You can't take these negative emotions into the kingdom. So if they are present your access is denied.

God will not hear your prayers if you don't forgive. I know it sounds harsh considering some of the things you have been through but the truth hurts.

Matthew 18:21-35 (MSG)

A Story About Forgiveness

21 At that point Peter got up the nerve to ask, "Master, how many times do I forgive a brother or sister who hurts me? Seven?"

22 Jesus replied, "Seven! Hardly. Try seventy times seven.

23-25 "The kingdom of God is like a king who decided to square accounts with his servants. As he got under way, one servant was brought before him who had run up a debt of a hundred thousand dollars. He couldn't pay up, so the king ordered the man, along with his wife, children, and goods, to be auctioned off at the slave market.

26-27 "The poor wretch threw himself at the king's feet and begged, 'Give me a chance and I'll pay it all back.' Touched by his plea, the king let him off, erasing the debt.

28 "The servant was no sooner out of the room when he came upon one of his fellow servants who owed him ten dollars. He seized him by the throat and demanded, 'Pay up. Now!'

29-31 "The poor wretch threw himself down and begged, 'Give me a chance and I'll pay it all back.' But he wouldn't do it. He had him arrested and put in jail until the debt was paid. When the other servants saw this going on, they were outraged and brought a detailed report to the king.

32-35 "The king summoned the man and said, 'You evil servant! I forgave your entire debt when you begged me for mercy. Shouldn't you be compelled to be merciful to your fellow servant who asked for mercy?' The king was furious and put the screws to the man until he paid back his entire debt. And that's exactly what my Father in heaven is going to do to each one of you who doesn't forgive unconditionally anyone who asks for mercy."

A parable is a story that represents the kingdom of God. Hopefully you are seeing the point. One servant owed a great deal of money, but pleaded for forgiveness. Yet he would not bestow that same mercy to another, even though he owed a greater debt.

When a person does not forgive the greater issue is that they are prideful. Pride will keep you out of the kingdom of God.

Luke 17:3 (NKJV)

3 Take heed to yourselves. If your brother sins against you,[a] rebuke him; and if he repents, forgive him.

Forgiveness is not, not standing up for yourself. The scripture above means if your brother offends you still rebuke him, meaning let him know about it. Rebuke means to express sharp disapproval or criticism of (someone) because of their behavior or actions. Then it says forgive him. So often we confuse passiveness with forgiveness. Forgiveness is not allowing people to take advantage of you, all in the name of being a super Christian.

The scripture means after you confront that person about their behavior, move on by forgiving them. There is a different between forgiveness, denial and repression. Denial means to deny or act as if the offense never happened or does not exist. Repression is to suppress or push down what you truly feel. Remember I said forgiveness can't be forced upon you. When people try to force forgiveness on you it either fits in the category of repression, oppression or denial.

When you pray, God won't hear your prayers if you have unforgiveness in your heart towards another.

Matthew 5:23-24 (NKJV)

23 Therefore if you bring your gift to the altar, and there remember that your brother has something against you, 24 leave your gift there before the altar, and go your way. First be reconciled to your brother, and then come and offer your gift.

God won't receive your offering if you have unforgiveness in your heart towards a brother.

Remember our Father in heaven forgives. In fact while He was in the process of being murdered He forgave.

Luke 23:34 (NKJV)

34 Then Jesus said, "Father, forgive them, for they do not know what they do."[a]

And they divided His garments and cast lots.

Jesus knows what it is like to be humiliated, abused, misused, misunderstood, beaten, and wrongfully accused. Yet He forgave.

Forgiveness is not easy; most people don't hold grudges over simply offenses. Often times it is the person closes to you that will hurt you the most. No matter how hard it is, remember it is possible.

We make the decision to forgive, Holy Spirit does the work. There are some sins against humanity that are simply unbearable and unthinkable. There are some offenses that without the presence of the Holy Spirit we will never overcome, due to how emotionally damaging it can be.

Without forgiveness there is no true repentance.

The definition of unforgiveness is simple it means to not forgive. It means to carry the weight of yesterday's hurts into our today. It means to carry the heavy burden of resentment, bitterness, anger, rage, hurt, turmoil, fear, violence and hatred, because of someone else's offense towards you. It means to carry resentment

To forgive means to let go of the heavy burden of resentment, bitterness, anger, rage, hurt, turmoil, and fear.

Which one do you want? You can never have peace, with unforgiveness in your heart.

Finally a quote by Kagen Salmansohn, "Forgiveness is a process. Forgiveness is not approval of the offender's wrong doing. It is not viewing what they did as less harmful than it truly was. And it's not about giving the offender a "free pass" to keep on doing wrong actions against you. Forgiveness is about recognizing that staying in resentment creates an "active echo" of the pain the offender caused. By saying that the awful offense is "beyond forgiving" you give them continued power over you. Forgiveness begins with the mind recognizing that there's truthful logic in how the past cannot be changed, but happily the present and future can be. Eventually forgiveness progresses to the heart with the heart deciding it will no longer allow the offender's pain to take permanent residence in your heart. Yes it is a process, but eventually the mind and heart together recognize that the choice to forgive is both logical and spiritually liberating.

Forgiveness doesn't excuse their behavior. Forgiveness prevents their behavior from destroying your heart.

Quote by www.beyondordinary.com

Excerpt from: *Healing The Heart Through Forgiveness by Samaria M Colbert*

Again in the inner healing session you must teach the counselee what forgiveness is, and how it will work to heal their hearts. Then lead them into a pray of forgiveness.

Chapter 6

Mother and Father Wounds

Psalm 27:10 (NKJV)

10 When my father and my mother forsake me,

Then the Lord will take care of me.

We cannot leave the discussion about roots of bitterness without talking about mother and father wounds. This particular area of bitterness is so important that an entire chapter is dedicated to this form of bitterness.

Let start with a few examples of how mother and father wounds impact an individual. Before we get started it is important to note the roles of mother and fathers in our lives. Fathers are to provide, protect, and give identify. Mother comfort, encourage and nurture. Let's look at an example of how this manifest within the counselee.

John and his wife Janice have only been married for a year. They thought they knew each other before they married. They were both raised in church. Shortly after getting married John and Janice began to experience marital problems. John would become upset with her if she didn't do a small thing, like call back immediately after a missed call. John expected Janice to be at his beck and call immediately. He expected to know where she was at all times. Janice began feeling quite resentful towards John almost immediately. When he was a tyrant over not hearing from her immediately, Janice was boiling mad, but she never said anything to John about his inappropriate behavior. At last, they met at the counselor's office because they were on the verge of separating just nine months into their marriage.

What does the counselor do?

This is is about how mother wounds and father wounds present themselves within individuals who show up for inner healing counseling sessions. You may not see it on the surface but what is going on is the unresolved mother and father wounds.

Mother and father wounds are not limited to married couples, in fact, we see mother and father wounds in single individuals as well.

Back to the young couple. You may be asking how does it relate to mother and father wounds? It is simple when they meet with the counselor who focuses on inner healing; the counselor again must use the gifts of the spirit. The counselor must ask, each of them what about their upbringing. The counselor must ask what was their father like and what was their mother like.

This is because of we each repeat patterns from our childhood. Our parents teach us how we are going to interact with our future spouses based upon their interaction with us and each other.

For example, I counseled a couple where the husband was very passive. He never stood up for the kids in school issues, for his wife, he barely worked. Her issue was that she was in so many words waiting for him to grow up and be a man. She was being forced to take on the role of mother and father when in reality they had been married for more than eighteen years. She had been forced to become the leader.

As we further explored, I began to ask him specifically about his parents; I wanted to focus on the relationship with his mother in particular. It turns out his mother was very domineering and controlling. His father was very passive and never spoke up for him or his siblings. The roles were very much reversed. What was sad was that he met a lovely young woman who was not domineering and controlling. She didn't have the best upbringing, but she had more of a balanced upbringing. Her parents were concerned about her, but not controlling.

Are you seeing this? The couple that I counseled the husband was simply interacting with women and in particularly his wife, the only way he had been taught to do. He was simply repeating the patterns from his childhood. He literarily didn't know any different. This was a recurring theme within our counseling sessions. At times it was very difficult to counsel him in particular because he had a hard time even talking to me. I had to point out the husband role, point out patterns that were repeated from childhood, and then give him therapeutic homework to practice more assertiveness, in different life scenarios.

Barriers to his recovery included that his mother was still very controlling and manipulating. She repeatedly kept intervening in their marriage and talk bad about his wife when she wouldn't allow herself to be manipulated by her.

The mother in law, his mother, was a modern day Jezebel. This is why we have to uncover and delve into mother and father wounds.

No, go back to the scenario that we started off with. By the way, the young couple that we started with was fictional. Before we move forward, I want you to consider what maybe the mother and father wounds in their relationship.

Before go further I want you to begin to hypothesize what do you think the young couples mother and fathers wounds were.

How would you approach them as their counselor?

Let mc give you a few clues.

As stated you would want to ask them about their upbringing.

What was their individual childhood like?

What were their parents like?

Go into detail about the mother and father.

Was the father in the home? This significant because if a man in particular has never gone through the process of healing before marriage he will relate to his mother the same way he relates to his wife. If the father was not in the home, the mother was the go getter, the one who got things done. She was the strong one who did everything. There is nothing wrong with a strong woman. It becomes a problem in marriage if the man relates to his wife, the same way he relates to his mother. Because a single mother will take on a role that a married wife should not. How does he relate to other men? Does he walk in his authority as a man? Or is he a modern day Ahab. For those that don't know Ahab was a passive fearful man, who submitted to his wife. He was a emasculated man, he had the position of a king but the character of a wimpy man.

This is a spirit. When a man is raised by a single woman, he learns to submit to a woman, and rightfully so she is his mother and has authority over him. Again this is not the role of a wife. In marriage, the wife is a partner, a co-contributor to the plan of God. The wife submits to the husband's authority. I know I am messing you up with this, but this is scripture.

No real woman of God wants a man who isn't a man. She doesn't want a man she can control. A woman wants a man that walks in divine authority and dominion; he is confident in who he is. No real woman wants a man that she has to mold and make into who he is called to be. That is out of order.

Hopefully, you have thought more about the young couple. So here is the answer. As it turns out John's mother was very manipulative and controlling. John hated growing up with his mother. He didn't become a modern day Ahab; he took on the characteristics of his mother. He had a deep hatred for women growing up, but he never knew it. He made an inner vow that he would never marry a woman like his mother. He would never allow a woman to control or manipulate him. The complete opposite happened. John never forgave his mother. A root of bitterness grew in him, and he ended up being the very thing he hated.

Janice on the other hand was raised by her parents. Her mother was extremely passive and avoided confrontation at any cost. Although her parents had more of a healthy relationship. She still took on the characteristics of her mother.

Let me pause here, oftentimes individuals take on characteristics of one parent more so than the other. It has nothing to do with favoritism. It has more to do with personality types. When I was growing up, people said I was more like my father because I was quiet and observant. I walked in wisdom even as a small child much like my dad. While my other sisters had more of an outgoing personality like my mother. My point is yes children take on one or more characteristics of both parents; it is not uncommon for an individual to relate to or take on the characteristics of one parent.

I had a client who I counseled; she told me how her sister who was only two years older than her was just like her mother in personality. While she was just like her father in personality, she would hang out with her father for hours doing the more masculine type of activities, where her sister spent more time with her mother.

Back to our young wife, Janice. Janice took on the characteristics of her mother. She was walked in wisdom, kindness, and grace but never stood up for herself. She feared confrontation at all cost. So when her husband was ranting and raging, she just kept it all in. She finally had enough and was on her way out of the door to end the marriage. The sad thing was she never talked to him about how she felt. Can you blame her? Before you decide to leave a marriage, you should have at least tried to talk about and work through the problems. This is hard to do when you have someone who won't talk for fear of confrontation.

So what does the inner healing counselor do? We already discussed what questions to ask. You have to identify the patterns from childhood and point them out. You have to teach them principles of mother and father wounds. You have to teach them about how we relate to our spouses based upon how our parents interacted with each other.

A word of warning don't be alarmed if you get resistance, when you start talking about families of origin and parents, some people can get defensive. With the one couple I counseled the husband wasn't getting it, so I finally had to tell him, that with all do respect it sounds like his mother was controlling and manipulative.

After that you must be led by the Holy Spirit to begin to pray healing prayers over their marriage, they may need to repent and ask God and each other for forgiveness. You may have to pray the prayer renouncing generational curses. Again you always contract for more counseling sessions because as I repeatedly have said and will continue to say, you can't remove something old without introducing something new. You have to teach them principles of healthy marriage from God's perspective. Remember I said when we have patterns of behavior that are in us, they can be hard to break without the help of the Holy Spirit.

Before we end this chapter and move on to the next, let us look at another example of mother and father wounds.

Barry is a 38 year old, male. He has been in and out of trouble due to the assault on a female. Barry has been in a relationship with a particular woman for over ten years, and they have two boys ages 5 and 8. On the outside, they look like a beautiful family. She is a business owner with her own hair salon. He owns his own mechanical shop. They own a beautiful home together, and their children are always dressed in the latest updated clothes. After the police have been called to the home multiple times. There is now an active court order barring Barry and his girlfriend from being within 50 yards of one another. His girlfriend is still in the home with the kids. He has been court ordered to attend anger management. She has been court ordered to seek out counseling. The children have their own separate counselor and have been diagnosed with post-traumatic stress disorder.

Barry shows up at your door because he wants to get his anger management sessions over with so he can comply with the courts and be reunited with his family.

Where do you begin? Before we move forward what do you think are some of the inner wounds, inner vows, and roots of bitterness that Barry may have. You know that something is going on based upon the brief history, you haven't even met with him.

What do you think could be the answer?

This is going to get complicated. Before you even meet with Barry, you are not even sure that he wants to counsel. What is his motivation for coming? Does he want to dive deep into his issues or is he just trying to meet the court requirements?

Let me help you.

As a Christian inner healing counselor, you would not wait until he gets to your office before you start praying about how to approach him. You don't know if he is receptive. Is he guarded, is he defensive?

As you pray for divine strategies BEFORE you ever meet with him, you are going to have to seek divine guidance from the Holy Spirit. He will not tell you the whole story or everything; Holy Spirit will give you something. It may be a small piece, but it is something.

Then you meet with him. From an administrative perspective, you would start with paper work, I have client's fill out a demographic form, I get their insurance information because I am a licensed mental health therapist how I get paid for services rendered is through the insurance. I start with an assessment.

It depends on what your credentials or background is. If you are credentialed in the mental health field, you start with assessments. However, you may not be required to start with an assessment or paperwork if you are a licensed pastoral counselor or a licensed clinical Christian counselor. If this is the case, I encourage you to have some kind of formal intake packet for the consumers to complete. Also, have ways to document the inner healing sessions. I use an electronic system called, therapynotes.com. Even if you don't bill insurance I would highly recommend, it helps to keep track of your sessions, what was talked about and the plan of action for the next session, and the plan for treatment. Remember I have stated multiple times that inner healing is not a onetime session, but a contract for sessions over a specific time. There is another one that is useful called theranest.com.

Both can be used for counselors who don't bill insurance and those that do.

My point when you identify how and why the consumer is coming into your office, it is important that you document your interactions. Particularly for Barry because he is mandated by the court to attend sessions. Make sure you are approved to see Barry if you're not credentialed as a mental health counselor.

In the case of court appointed clients, you must have forms that specify that you are able to release information. We call this the confidentiality release form.

Remember all sessions are confidential in accordance to laws that govern HIPPA. You can be held liable if you release information to any source without the consumers consent.

So Barry comes in and basically starts by filling out paperwork. Paperwork consist of a demographics form, (Names, date, address, contact, insurance, emergency contact, reason for seeking services.)

For those who are also mental health counselors you may want to have a statement of faith form. Meaning some kind of memorandum statement about the organizations statement of faith, and have the counselees sign that they are aware of the organizations stance and are okay with continuing to receive counseling services with this agency.

Then you will complete brief assessment evaluation Barry's history.

What questions do you need to focus on with Barry? This is easy because we have went over specific questions previously.

You want to ask Barry what was his childhood like. What were his parents like? What was his father like? What was his mother like? For Barry you may want to ask about specific relationships he has had in the past? How does he relate to women in general? Does he have mother and father wounds?.

Well you are in session with Barry, he appears to be a bright man with a lot of potential but he has a chip on his shoulder. He appears to be abrasive and guarded. I have to put this in here because every counselee that you meet may not be happy to be there. A good counselor knows how to engage a client in such a authentic way they let their guard down some and slowly begin to open up to you. What I have found helpful is to just be kind, don't be judgmental, meet people where they are. Most people know that they are wrong before they walk through the door, they are not interested in a lecture.

In the case of Barry I would just start asking him about his likes, what he does, what he is passionate about, and then his family? I would point out his positives, while telling him that we clearly have somethings to work on. I would find away to let Barry know that I am not against him, realistically we will work together on change, but he has to be the main participant of his own healing. I am just the helper, he is the expert of his own life.

There is not an exact wordage or exact way to approach it these are just my suggestions based upon my experience. Remember we said earlier that it is the Holy Spirit who speaks through us. It is God who draws people, and unhardens the hearts of man. You may not be able to get through to Barry but the Holy Spirit can. You have to lean on Him.

Okay I will no longer leave you in suspense. As it turns out Barry was raised in a home where he witnessed his father beat on his mother repeatedly. Ironically Barry vows that he would never be like his father. His parents stayed together for over 24 years, in fact they are still married to this day. Barry witnessed the police coming in at out of his home growing up. Barry was removed by child protective services between the ages of 11 and 13. His parents were mandated to attending parenting courses, and their own separate counselors. The parents complied with all the CPS requirements he and his sister were returned to their home. Things were good no violence for a while, but the domestic violence returned. Barry repeatedly witnessed his father beat on his mother. As the time kept going on he got angrier and angrier, he never was given proper treatment, he just held his feelings in. Finally things came to headway, when Barry was 16. Barry then bigger than his father, witnessed his mother being beat up by his father. Barry had enough. He finally intervened between his father and mother. Barry began beating his father up. There was no stopping Barry and his sister called the police to get Barry off his father.

At the age of 16 Barry was charged with assault, and was sent to juvenile detention. Ironically his parents never came to visit him, his mother did attempt to secretly call Barry when his father was not present, but was not able to because his father had very strict control over his mother.

Eventually at a court hearing, Barry was able to articulate why he beat his father up. There was documentation of his history with CPS regarding the domestic violence within the home and all charges were dismissed. Although Barry was mandated to attend counseling for the trauma he never followed.

Barry never returned home. Instead he dropped out of high school, he ended of getting his GED. He attended community college where he got an associates degree in mechanical science, he started his own business.

Although on the surface Barry was doing well and had overcame. He never overcame the hurt of seeing his mother beat up all those years and there was nothing he could do about it. Then on top of that when he finally did do something about it he felt great rejection related to his own mother never coming to court, calling him regularly or visiting him while he was in juvenile detention. He felt a great deal of rejection. He felt angry at his sister for calling the police, but he understood that she was trying to help him. Barry was so full of rage he would have killed his father, and the charges would have been much greater if he had a murder charge on his record.

Barry had deep seated unresolved hurts, wounds, rage and anger that has never been dealt with.

We have gone over many principles of inner healing so I won't give you the answers to this one, but in session you would want to know.

What was the inner vows he made? (hint: I already said one of them.)

What was the bitterroots?

What are his mother and father wounds?

What are the major strongholds that is impacting Barry now?

How can forgiveness begin to heal? Remember Barry can't control how he was raised. He can't erase the past, he can decide to heal his heart through forgiveness.

If Barry was your counselee or you have a counselee similar to Barry you will have to minister and teach him the principles of forgiveness. I recommend that for a homework assignment you give Barry the book *Healing the Heart Through Forgiveness* by Samaria M Colbert

Other things that you may not know is that Barry had deep seated resentment towards his mother that turned to hate. Barry resented how his mother never left his father. Barry's resentment turned to hatred. Barry had deep seated hatred to all women as a result. One of the reasons why Barry is so angry at his girlfriend is because he hates women. He loved his mother and hated her at the same time. Which translated to how he relates to women now. Again he loves his girlfriend but hates her at the same time. When he sees her, he sees his mother.

This is an interesting case. We don't know about the girlfriend.

Some may ask can inner healing be rendered to someone that is not a Christian? Technically Barry is not a Christian. He is committing fornication by living with a woman who is not his wife.

The answer is yes you can. You don't have to be a Christian to receive inner healing treatment. A person need only be open to the biblical principles of inner healing. However I must say that being a Christian and having Christ in your heart is really when the change begins. It is my hope that through the minister of inner healing if you have someone who is not a Christian, as you begin to do the work as the vessel rendering inner healing, that the person would be drawn to receive a relationship with Jesus Christ. Inner Healing work will not work as effectively if a person is not in Christ.

What I am saying is that just because a person is not a Christian don't turn them away from the counseling session, you are just the person they need to meet with. Remember if we lift Christ up He will draw others to Him. It is our responsibility to be the willing vessels that He uses, He does the drawing.

John 12:32 (NKJV)

32 And I, if I am lifted up from the earth, will draw all peoples to Myself."

Romans 5:8New King James Version (NKJV)

One final point before we leave this chapter is that in the case of Barry you will notice the reason he came in was for anger management, but with further exploration his symptoms are more related to unresolved trauma.

Just because a person comes into session with one particular problem doesn't mean that is what you are going to be counseling them for. In the case of Barry had we simply taken out our anger management techniques and begun to address the symptoms we would have never gotten to the root of the problem that was really triggering the anger and rage.

Most of the time and I do mean most of the time, what a person identifies as the problem with further evaluation will not be the root problem. Many people are oblivious to how the past is impacting them. Someone may be experiencing marriage problems but with further exploration what they are really struggling with mother and father wounds of abandonment that is impacting their today. Another one that I get a lot of is a person seeking services of chronic anxiety, however when I deal with the root they really experiencing self-doubt, insecurity and the fruit of rejection that is rooted in childhood. You can't take what you initially see at first value. Remember always explore further, we must peel back the layers and get to the root.

Chapter 7

Unconscious Defense Mechanism

2 Corinthians 10:5-7 (NKJV)

5 casting down arguments and every high thing that exalts itself against the knowledge of God, bringing every thought into captivity to the obedience of Christ, 6 and being ready to punish all disobedience when your obedience is fulfilled.

In the counseling sessions you will be confronted with individual barriers and strongholds that if not dealt with the counselee can get stuck. Getting stuck is where the individual stops making progress within the counseling session, and in some cases begins to decompensate. We must explore the unconscious defense mechanisms. This is something you need to be particularly aware of when counseling someone who is in ministry.

Before we go further we must take time to consider some psychological terms that will be important to our study in this particularly chapter. It will all make sense as we go through this chapter.

Terms we will discuss is masking personality, co-dependency, dysfunctional family patterns. Dysfunctional family roles, intergenerational family coping mechanisms, familiar spirits, reversal roles such as child-mothers, child fathers, emotional incest, unmet emotional needs. Some of you may be familiar with some of the terms that we have identified, now let's define them. I will give you the secular definition and the biblical definition.

First let us define exactly what a defense mechanism it.

A defense mechanism is an unconscious psychological mechanism that reduces anxiety arising from unacceptable or potentially harmful stimuli.

https://en.wikipedia.org/wiki/Defence_mechanisms

A defense mechanism is often unconscious mental process (such as repression) that makes possible compromise solutions to personal problems.

https://www.merriamwebster.com/dictionary/defense%20mechanism

So in laymen's term a unconscious defense mechanism is a invisible, unconscious term for an individual's attempt to avoid emotional pain by unconscious words, acts, deeds, or internal responses. Emphasis on the term unconscious. Unconscious means not knowing, unaware, not knowing or perceiving.

Have you ever been driving, and you got to your destination but didn't remember the drive? Maybe you have taken that same road so many times that your mind was elsewhere while you drove to your destination. I do not recommend this of course but am using this as an example. Have you ever known someone who was unconscious or in coma? It is said that they can hear what is being said but have no ability to respond.

That mind is like a computer it remembers but sometimes with painful memories it will hide things so deep you don't know that they are there but they are very real. This will be present at times when dealing with trauma survivors, their minds will hide the memory of trauma's to the point where the counselee doesn't remember. Yet when assessing for post-traumatic stress disorder they meet all the criteria or have many of the long term affects for trauma that they don't remember.

Often times a person may not be aware that they are using unconscious unhealthy defense mechanisms. Most of the unconscious defense mechanisms are unhealthy for us, we use them to get through what we are going through. The good news is God has a better way. Unconscious defense mechanisms become strongholds if we leave them unchecked.

Now about those terms let's go back and define them.

Masking personality-Masking is a process in which an individual changes or "masks" their natural personality to conform to social pressures, abuse, and/or harassment.

https://en.wikipedia.org/wiki/Masking_(personality)

Examples of this can be found in teenagers that conform to social pressures so they take on the personality of their peers. Say a young boy who is a straight A student, but he doesn't want to be perceived as a nerd or he is teased by his peers so he takes another persona to be excepted. Maybe his grades drop, maybe he starts acting as if he doesn't care.

I mentioned something about minsters. You will find this evident if you are counseling someone who is in ministry. They maybe not be fully honest about how they feel for fear of being misjudged. Often as Christians we are taught that we are not supposed to be afraid, anxious or depressed. I agree that we the Holy Spirit gives us peace and joy. However we still struggle with these things in our humanity. Yes God can and will deliver, but He won't deliver you from a problem that you won't acknowledge. This is very important counselors because you can't counsel someone who can't admit that they have a problem.

If there is no problem to confront with the word of God, then there is no resolution.

Often times we are taught this name it and claim it mentality. That is if we name it the negative emotions, and claim it then it becomes a part of us. Don't get me wrong there is some truth in that if you say, you are broke then you are broke. If you say you are going to lose your mind then you will lose your mind. The key is in the purpose.

You and the counselee are not to claim something that is not there, you are to identify the problem. You are naming the problem, **with the purpose of healing**

from it. You are identifying what the problem is so that you can know what actions to take.

Examples of this can be found in the word of God.

Luke 8:30 (NKJV)

30 Jesus asked him, saying, "What is your name?"

And he said, "Legion," because many demons had entered him.

Jesus was not claiming a demons spirit, no He was identifying what was already there in order for real deliverance to take place within the person. So that is why Jesus asked the demon what his name was. He wasn't bringing the demon to the man he was simply using discernment to identify what was already there.

That is what inner healing counselors do, we are not getting you to claim a spirit or a diagnosis, we are simply identifying what is already there so real deliverance can take place. What we didn't read in Luke was that after this Jesus cast out the demon called Legion. I encourage you to read further in your own time.

This is so important because the church culture as we know it now there is a distrust for doctors, lawyers and counselors. I have lost count as to how many times I have heard a pastor make statement about doctors and counselors in rude demeaning ways.

Friends doctors, lawyers, psychiatrist, therapist are not your enemy. They are not the churches enemy. If that was the case then why was Luke a physician allowed to write a testament in the bible? Why does proverbs talk multiple times about counselors? Why are lawyers presented in the bible as well?

As counselors you will be confronted with church culture in the counselees you see, it is okay to be led by the Holy Spirit to confront these strongholds, because if a person doesn't get over their hiccup with help agents it can delay and in some case stop the healing process. There is so much more that I can say about this topic but I must me move on. Maybe one day in another book I will address this further.

I know I have repeatedly said this but before we move to the next defense mechanism I must say this again, you cannot get healed or delivered from what you don't acknowledge.

The next defense mechanism is codependency. Co-dependency is excessive emotional or psychological reliance on a partner, typically a partner who requires support due to an illness or addiction. In other words codependence is being so emotionally, mentally and spiritually intertwined with another human being so that the individual cannot make decisions without the person or their emotional state is interwoven in an unhealthy way to another person.

According to webMD. Co-dependency is;

Being unable to find satisfaction in your life outside of a specific person.

Recognizing unhealthy behaviors in your partner but staying.

Giving support to your partner at the cost of your own mental, emotional, and physical health.

http://www.webmd.com/sex-relationships/features/signs-of-a-codependent-relationship#1

Remember I said that the world takes biblical principles gives it a different name. In Christendom we refer to codependency as a soul tie. A soul tie is a unhealthy, spiritual connection to the soul of another person.

Prophet Kris Vallotton gives us 7 characteristics of someone that is in a soul tie.

7 SIGNS THAT YOU HAVE AN UNHEALTHY SOUL TIE:

1. You are in a physically, and/or emotionally, and/or spiritually abusive relationship, but you "feel" so attached to them that you refuse to cut off the connection and set boundaries with them.

2. You have left a relationship (maybe long ago), but you think about the other person obsessively (you can't get them out of your mind).

3. Whenever you do anything – make a decision, have a conversation with someone etc., you "feel" like this person is with you or watching you.

4. When you have sex with someone else (hopefully your husband or wife), you can hardly keep yourself from visualizing the person you have a soul tie with.

5. You take on the negative traits of the person that your soul is tied to and carry their offenses whether or not you actually agree with them.

6. You defend your right to stay in a relationship with the person that your soul is tied to, even though it is

negatively effecting or even destroying the important relationships in your life (husband, wife, kids, leaders, etc.)

7. You have simultaneous experiences and/or "moods" as the person your soul is tied to. This can even include sickness, accidents, addictions etc.1 Corinthians 6:15 – Do you not know that the one who joins himself to a prostitute is one body with her? For He says, "THE TWO SHALL BECOME ONE FLESH."

http://krisvallotton.com/7-signs-of-an-unhealthy-soul-tie/

Again we didn't go into more specifics about codependency, but the same characteristics of codependency is the exact same as soul ties. In fact we could take out the word soul tie, and put in co-dependency and get the same definition and long term affects.

This is so important to us as inner healing counselors because the world have a basic knowledge of treatment for co-dependency but we in Christ have the answer.

Co-dependency really is a spiritual condition it must be addressed from the spirit realm. The secular counseling community cannot address it as a spiritual issue because they are not spiritual. Remember in Christ we have the answers to what the world needs.

This is also where the counselor must be well versed in deliverance ministry because at some point the soul tie when a person stays in this relationship too long, will take on demonic entities. Again the secular counseling world has no idea how to combat demonic warfare.

The Christian counselor must understand how to address and do spiritual surgery on the counselee.

We have already defined this term in a previous chapter. The secular world calls this, transgenerational trauma. Transgenerational trauma that is transferred from the first generation of trauma survivors to the second and further generations of offspring of the survivors via complex post-traumatic stress disorder mechanisms.

In economics, the cycle of poverty is the "set of factors or events by which poverty, once started, is likely to continue unless there is outside intervention".[1]

The cycle of poverty has been defined as a phenomenon where poor families become impoverished for at least three generations, i.e. for enough time that the family includes no surviving ancestors who possess and can transmit the intellectual, social, and cultural capital necessary to stay out of or change their impoverished condition. In calculations of expected generation length and ancestor lifespan, the lower median age of parents in these families is offset by the shorter lifespans in many of these groups.

https://en.wikipedia.org/wiki/Cycle_of_poverty

We defined these terms early as generational curses and we made reference to the scripture in Deuteronomy that states that God would release a curse to the third and fourth generation. We also read how other non-Christian counselors defines this term as patterns and pathologies.

Deuteronomy 5:10

…… I will bring the curse of a father's sins upon even the third and fourth generation of the children of those who hate me;…..

It is by no accident that the cycles are about three generations to the cycle of poverty, but scripture says that God would release a curse to the third generation.

On to the next:

Parentification is the process of role reversal whereby a child is obliged to act as parent to their own parent. In extreme cases, the child is used to fill the void of the alienating parent's emotional life.[1]

Two distinct modes of parentification have been identified technically: instrumental parentification and emotional parentification. Instrumental parentification involves the child completing physical tasks for the family, such as looking after a sick relative, paying bills, or providing assistance to younger siblings that would normally be provided by a parent. Emotional parentification occurs when a child or adolescent must take on the role of a confidant or mediator for (or between) parents or family members.[2]

Some call this parentified child syndrome, this is when the child takes on the role of the parent. They either become the mother or father to their parent. Children can take on the responsibility of caring for their parents as if they were the parent. Or they take on the responsibility of being a parent to their younger siblings.

https://en.wikipedia.org/wiki/Parentification

I first saw this with my own eyes almost 15 years ago. I went to Zimbabwe and saw children ran homes. Either the parent was sick and unable to care for the child, or the parents had died from AIDS and the oldest child was found to be taking care of their younger siblings.

In America we see more of this when parents are addicted to drugs and alcohol. The child takes on the responsibility of raising the younger siblings or raising parents.

Even when there is no substance abuse, we typically see the child have to raise their parents, as the parent takes on the child role. I am not referring to the end of life care that we see, when the parents become elderly and their child takes on the role of caring for the parent.

As counselors you will see this manifest in relationships. The counselee may not see this as a problem until they get into serious relationships. T.D Jakes came out with a movie some years ago entitled:

Jumping The Broom. In the movie the main character is getting married, but his mother tries to sabotage the relationship because she feels as though she may lose a son. The story is fictional but the scenarios are not all fictional.

We see this typically in single parent homes. This is where the son was raised by his mother. Somewhere along the way, the son takes on the role of the husband to his mother, minus the sexual intimacy of course. Other than that every other role is the same.

This becomes a problem because eventual the man wants to get married and have a family of his own. He then meets a woman who he identifies he wants to marry. In some cases if the issue is not dealt with it becomes a bigger issue in their marriage. The issue is that the mother doesn't see the wife or fiancé as her gaining a daughter, she sees the woman as competition. The reason why she sees the woman as competition is because the son has taken on the emotional role, and in some cases the burden of the husband. Mom doesn't have a man, therefore her son becomes her man. I call this emotional incest. We know what incest is but for the sake of the text let's go there.

Incest is sexual relations between people classed as being too closely related to marry each other. Incest is the crime of having sexual intercourse with a parent, child, sibling, or grandchild. Notice it says this is a crime. In the kingdom of God emotional incest is just as much a crime as physical incest. This is why the bible says when a man is grown and married he has to leave and cleave.

Emotional incest, also known as covert incest, is a dynamic that occurs in parenting where the parent seeks emotional support through their child that should be sought through an adult relationship. Although the effects of emotional incest can be similar to those resulting from physical incest, the term does not encompass sexual abuse.

https://www.goodtherapy.org/blog/emotional-covert-incest-when-parents-make-their-kids-partners-0914165

Covert incest, also known as emotional incest, is a style of parenting in which a parent looks to their child for the emotional support that would be normally provided by another adult.[1] The effects of covert incest on children when they become adults are thought to mimic actual incest, although to a lesser degree.

Covert incest is described as occurring when a parent is unable or unwilling to maintain a relationship with another adult and forces the emotional role of a spouse onto their child instead.[8] The child's needs are ignored and instead the relationship exists solely to meet the needs of the parent[1][3] and the adult may not be aware of the issues created by their actions.[11

https://en.wikipedia.org/wiki/Covert_incest

Scripture is clear about the stance of marital relationships.

Genesis 2:24 (KJV)

24 Therefore shall a man leave his father and his mother, and shall cleave unto his wife: and they shall be one flesh.

Leave and cleave is not just a physical state of being, but a mental and emotional state.

I am going to ask you a silly question that I am sure you know the answer to but I need you to think about it. What do you call it when a man starts engaging in a relationship with another woman who is not his wife?

Adultery, is voluntary sexual intercourse between a married person and a person who is not his or her spouse.

When an individual continues in an emotional incestual relationship with someone who is not their spouse in Christendom we consider this emotional adultery. It doesn't matter who it is.

An emotional affair (emotional adultery) can be defined as: "A relationship between a person and someone other than (their) spouse (or lover) that affects the level of intimacy, emotional distance and overall dynamic balance in the marriage. The role of an affair is to create emotional distance in the marriage."

https://en.wikipedia.org/wiki/Emotional_affair

The term often describes a bond between two people that mimics the closeness and emotional intimacy of a romantic relationship while never being physically consummated.

An emotional affair is sometimes referred to as an affair of the heart. An emotional affair may emerge from a friendship, and progress toward greater levels of personal intimacy and attachment. What distinguishes an emotional affair from a friendship is the assumption of emotional roles between the two participants that mimic of those of an actual relationship - with regards to confiding personal information and turning to the other person during moments of vulnerability or need.

https://en.wikipedia.org/wiki/Emotional_affair

As counselors we must understand these concepts. I know I may have offended some of you yet if we want people to come to full deliverance we can't be afraid to confront them with the truth. A wife and the mother don't have the same platform, they should not hold the exact same emotional space in a man's heart. A man shouldn't put his wife and his mother at the same place in his life. According to scripture a man has to leave where he was raised and be one with his wife. It doesn't say be one with his mother.

These breaches of boundaries creates emotional distance between the husband and wife, and if unchecked can lead to divorce. I highlighted the son mother role because that is what we tend to see more often, but you can see this in daughter father roles.

Again we tend to see it more in son mother roles because there is a long standing epidemic in our world today that woman are raising boys on their own. I am not suggesting that all single parents are like this, but it something that you will see in counseling sessions, particularly for couples who come in for Christian marriage counselor.

Relationships require healthy boundaries. A boundary is not the same as a wall. No one is asking a counselee to disown their parents, or the mother, we are teaching them the importance of boundaries. Boundaries are just that boundaries, unofficial and official rules about what should not be done, limits that define acceptable behavior.

Notice also the scripture say the husband is the head of his wife, it never said he was the head of his mother.

Ephesians 5:23 (KJV)

23 For the husband is the head of the wife, even as Christ is the head of the church: and he is the saviour of the body.

Another concept we need to talk about is unmet emotional needs. When we have unmet emotional needs we tend to revert back to unconscious defense mechanisms.

Just like we have physical needs for our wellbeing such as clothes, food, shelter. We have emotional needs.

Emotional need is a psychological or mental requirement of intrapsychic origin that usually centers on such basic feelings as love, fear, anger, sorrow, anxiety, frustration, and depression and involves the understanding, empathy, and support of one person for another.

Medical dictionary.thefreedictionary.com/emotional+need-

We learned concepts in graduate school about Maslow hierarchy of needs.

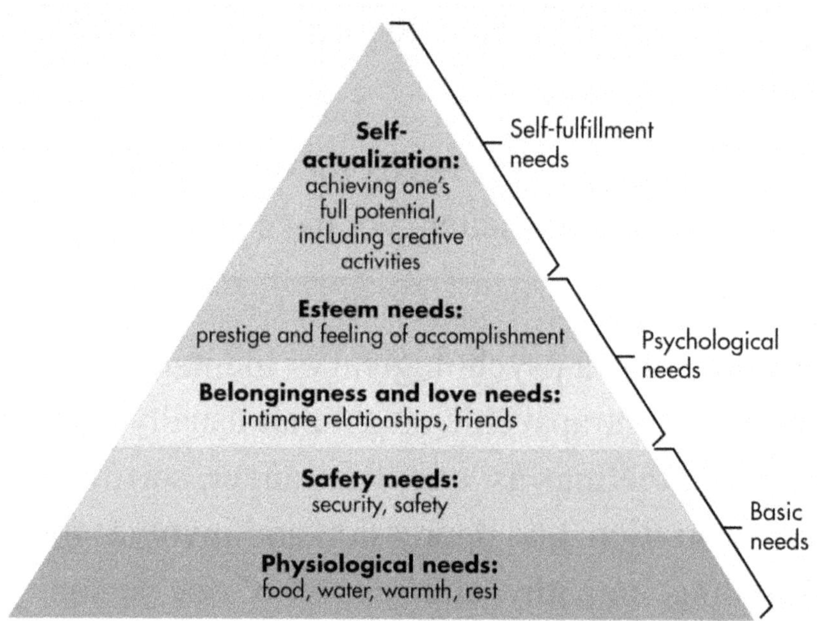

Notice in the diagram that basic needs were at the bottom, but as we go up the emotional needs are at the top. It tells us that as human beings we place a great deal of emphasis on emotional needs and when they are not met there are deficits in our lives.

It is my belief that what we are longing for really is for the Father. We were created to be fulfilled and to worship God. When we don't know Him or our relationship with Him is not there as it should be what we created is an emotional, mental and spiritual deficit.

So how does what we talked about play out as unconscious defense mechanism? These defense mechanism are what you the counselor will be confronted with in session.

1. Denial a person maybe the super spiritual saint who denies they have a problem while their life is falling apart.

2. Regression is when an individual reverts back to an earlier stage we discussed this in detail about child parents and emotional incest.

3. Acting out, in children or fits of rage in adults.

4. Dissociation, is when a person loses tract of time or places. They don't remember painful events this is present when counseling's those who have experienced severe sexual abuse and trauma.

5. Compartmentalization- when a person has two set of values. Examples being the pastor who preaches against sin in the church, but then turns around and cheats on his wife.

6. Projection-when an individual has unpleasant thoughts about themselves but instead of acknowledging it they project or displaces their feelings about themselves onto another.

7. Reaction Formation-converting unwanted thoughts into the opposite action. Examples being the woman who is so angry at how she is treated by her mother, she responds by being overly kind, allow herself to be manipulated and never speak up.

8. Repression-blocking unacceptable thoughts, feelings and impulses.

9. Displacement-similar to project, however the person redirects the thoughts, feelings and impulses of one person or object and takes it out on another. Examples being the man who is angry about how he is treated at work then goes home and takes it out on his wife and kids by beating them.

10. Intellectualization-you try to explain away with facts and figures. You find this within Christendom when a leader is caught in sin,

instead of humility admitting their wrong, they instead use scripture to justify their actions.

11.   Rationalization is making light of something. Examples being the person found caught in sin, and they make statement like, "well everybody does it, or no man can judge me but God."

12.   Undoing- trying to take back a unconscious behavior. In Christendom this is displayed with religious spirits who try to earn their way to heaven, or seek their works as their salvation.

13.   Procrastination is the action of delaying or postponing something. Saying, "I do it tomorrow and tomorrow never comes."

Proverbs 6:6-8 (KJV)

6 Go to the ant, thou sluggard; consider her ways, and be wise:

7 Which having no guide, overseer, or ruler,

8 Provideth her meat in the summer, and gathereth her food in the harvest.

Proverbs 6:4 (NIV)

4 Allow no sleep to your eyes,

no slumber to your eyelids.

14.	Passiveness-accepting or allowing what happens or what others do, without active response or resistance. Passiveness is really a demonic spirit, found in King Ahab that lives on today. See I Kings 17 and read through for scriptural references

15.	Aggressiveness-ready or likely to attack or confront; characterized. This presents itself when a person is angry, and masking hurt feelings. This person presents as very defensive and hard to confront even if it is done with great respect.

So how does the inner healing counselor address such a person. For these responses there is not a direct answer. Again you have to use the gifts of the spirit.

Timothy 4:2 (NKJV)

2 Preach the word! Be ready in season and out of season. Convince, rebuke, exhort, with all longsuffering and teaching.

2 Timothy 4:2 (KJV)

2 Preach the word; be instant in season, out of season; reprove, rebuke, exhort with all long suffering and doctrine.

There are other defense mechanisms that we won't have time to address. However when getting resistance from a counselee, you must use the Word, the Word, the Word of God. You must be led by the Holy Spirit. He is the answer. It is only the word of God that can pierce hardened hearts.

Hebrews 4:12 (KJV)

12 For the word of God is quick, and powerful, and sharper than any two edged sword, piercing even to the dividing asunder of soul and spirit, and of the joints and marrow, and is a discerner of the thoughts and intents of the heart.

The word of God pierces through all resistance.

Remember what I said, allow the Holy Spirit to take over, point out to the counselee where they are using a defense mechanism and confront them with the word. Pray for them continue to move forward with the inner healing sessions.

Chapter 8

Speak To Your Soul

Psalm 42:11 (NKJV)

11 Why are you cast down, O my soul?

And why are you disquieted within me?

Hope in God;

For I shall yet praise Him,

The help of my countenance and my God.

We cannot fully understand inner healing without understanding how the soul is an intricate part of our healing. We know that the body is made up of three parts. The mind is the part that processes information; the spirit is the invisible part of us that was created for eternity. Then there is the soul. The Hebrew definition word of the soul it nephesh, which means a living being. Our soul is a living being that dwells within the body. The Hebrew word for spirit is pneuma; to breathe, blow, primarily denotes the wind. Breath; the spirit which, like the wind, is invisible, immaterial, and powerful.

For man to be created, God breathed into man.

Genesis 2:7 (KJV)

7 And the Lord God formed man of the dust of the ground, and breathed into his nostrils the breath of life; and man became a living soul.

Notice when God breathed into man, he breathed into him life; then he became a living soul. This is very important; man cannot live without the breath of God in him. You can be alive and still dead spiritually when you have no relationship with God. Without God's breath, man cannot be a living soul. It will make sense as we go along.

The word for mind in the Hebrew means heart. It means lebab inner man, mind, will, heart. When God tells us to serve Him, He also includes every aspect of your being.

Luke 10:27 (KJV)

27 And he answering said, Thou shalt love the Lord thy God with all thy **heart**, and with all **thy soul**, and

with all thy strength, and with all **thy mind**; and thy neighbour as thyself.

I don't know about you, but I have studied a great deal on the mind in the counseling. We therapist, are taught how to implement what is called cognitive behavioral therapy. It means how the mind interprets information, which turns into what we believe about ourselves. Again another biblical concept that the world has taken. I am sure you have read the book by now Battlefield of the Mind by Joyce Meyers if you haven't I encourage you to read it. Then I have studied a great deal on the heart. In fact, I already told you about my book, *Healing The Heart Through Forgiveness.*

Nevertheless, I will admit I haven't read as much about the soul. It is like we don't understand the importance of the soul and we gloss over it. This chapter will highlight how we need to speak to our soul. I am not suggesting that it is any less important that the mind and the spirit if the scripture says that we have to love the Lord with all are heart, soul, and mind that is what it means. The reason I chose to highlight the soul is that it is so overlooked as stated and we have to understand the significance of the soul for our inner healing. There is a lot of information about the heart, and the mind, again in my opinion not as much about the soul. In fact, lets go back to the scripture we read in Psalms 42. Let's read it again before we read it; I want you to ask yourself who David was speaking to?

Psalm 42:11 (NKJV)

11 Why are you cast down, O my soul?

And why are you disquieted within me?

Hope in God;

For I shall yet praise Him,

The help of my countenance and my God.

If you look at the text very carefully, David is not talking to God. He is not only talking to himself he is talking to his soul. He is not only talking to his soul, he then changes gears and begins to encourage his soul.

He is saying, "soul why are you discouraged? Why are you so upset with me?" Then he goes and tells his soul what to do, "Hope in God." He is telling his soul what to do; then he is commanding his body to do something, "praise."

Why is this so important? Because your soul can be so discouraged, so down, that it decides to deteriorate, but your mind and your spirit have determined to live.

If you let your soul make the choices your mind, your body and your spirit will follow. You have to know how and when to command your soul to get it together.

Once again the world has taken a God concept renamed it and called it something different. We again give credit back to it's rightful owner God. The world has taken this concept and put it into a form of counseling called DBT Dialectal behavioral counseling. They teach the principle called the three wise minds.

Let us look at a diagram:

DBT Three Wise Minds

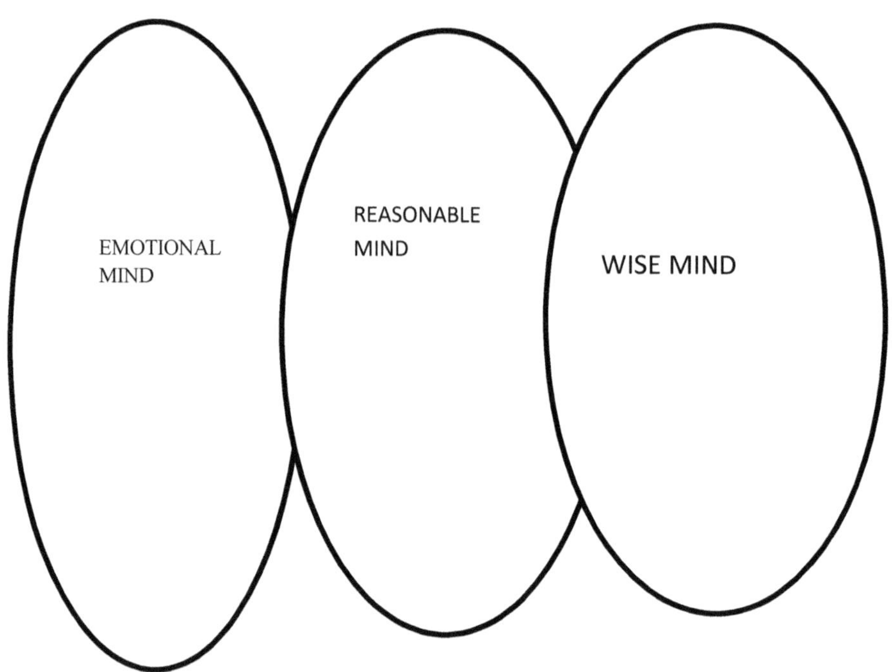

DBT Theorist believes that we have three minds. The emotional mind wants to make decisions based on the emotions. Emotions will lead you the wrong way. The reasonable mind asked questions and attempts to rethink what the emotional mind wants to do. The wise mind if allowed wants to make wise decisions. They use this concept for individuals who are impulsive have a personality disorder to regulate emotions. I am again not publicly endorsing DBT, in fact, DBT is based upon the Buddhist religion. However, I again showed you this diagram to show you how the world takes biblical concepts and calls it their own.

So what does the bible have to say? I am glad you asked.

We are spiritual beings, with a body, that has a soul. Similar to the three wise mind the soul always wants to lead. The soul is where the emotional mind is. We all have a spirit; we must submit our spirit to the Holy Spirit, we all have a soul. The soul part of us is what contempt's, ask questions begins to rationalize if it is not submitted to God, the body will follow, and the spirit will be dead. Hopefully, you see how this is similar. Again for this book, I am focusing on the soul, but there is so much to learn about how we operate. I have heard people say I am a spirit being, living in a body, that has a soul.

Let us look at other aspects of the soul.

- Your soul can be dead while your physical body and spirit are alive.
- The soul is what needs to be revived.

Revived means restored to life, consciousness, and awakening.

- The demonic attacks are against your soul because your soul will either spend eternity in heaven or hell. The enemy, satan is after your soul.
- You soul is what can be converted.

Psalm 19:7(KJV)

7 The law of the Lord is perfect, **converting the soul**: the testimony of the Lord is sure, making wise the simple.

- Your soul can be revived to life. Let's look at another example.

1 Kings 17:17-22 (KJV)

17 And it came to pass after these things, that the son of the woman, the mistress of the house, fell sick; and his sickness was so sore, that there was no breath left in him.

18 And she said unto Elijah, What have I to do with thee, O thou man of God? art thou come unto me to call my sin to remembrance, and to slay my son?

19 And he said unto her, Give me thy son. And he took him out of her bosom, and carried him up into a loft, where he abode, and laid him upon his own bed.

20 And he cried unto the Lord, and said, O Lord my God, hast thou also brought evil upon the widow with whom I sojourn, by slaying her son?

21 And he stretched himself upon the child three times, and cried unto the Lord, and said, **O Lord my God, I pray thee, let this child's soul come into him again.**

22 And the Lord heard the voice of Elijah; **and the soul of the child came into him again, and he revived.**

Did you catch that? The soul of the child came back again. Let's keep going.

- The soul experiences adversities.

Proverbs 10:3 (KJV)

3 The Lord will not suffer the soul of the righteous to famish: but he casteth away the substance of the wicked.

Psalm 40:14 (KJV)

Let them be ashamed and confounded together that seek after my soul to destroy it; let them be driven backward and put to shame that wish me evil.

- The Lord redeems the souls. No one else, no person, no entity can restore the soul only God can. You can't even redeem or own soul without God. People can encourage you, make you feel better with a kind word, but only God can redeem the soul, particularly after it has reached the depths of despair.

Psalm 34:22 (KJV)

22 The Lord redeemeth the soul of his servants: and none of them that trust in him shall be desolate.

- For God to restore my soul, my soul must belong to Him. You have to commit your soul to God. It doesn't mean that when you are a Christian, you won't experience a depressed or damaged soul. It does mean that because our soul belongs to Him, by our choosing, He has the responsibility to restore, redeem and heal what already belongs to Him.
- It is perfectly fine to speak to your soul as long as you are declaring the word of God. We don't

worship our soul as the secular word tells us. We don't find answers within our souls. Our souls are not mystical beings within us that have supernatural power. No these are secular teachings that are rooted in the demonic world, based upon humanistic theories. Our souls are a part of us that God created, that must be revived and recommitted back to its maker, God through Jesus Christ.

Psalm 35:3-4 (KJV)

3 Draw out also the spear, and stop the way against them that persecute me: **say unto my soul**, I am thy salvation.

4 Let them be confounded and put to shame that **seek after my soul**: let them be turned back and brought to confusion that devise my hurt.

- The soul can rejoice and experience joy.

Psalm 35:9 (KJV)

9 And my soul shall be joyful in the Lord: it shall rejoice in his salvation.

- The soul can be discouraged.

Psalm 42:5 (KJV)

5 Why art thou cast down, O my soul? and why art thou disquieted in me? Hope thou in God: for I shall yet praise him for the help of his countenance.

- The soul can grieve.

Judges 10:16 (KJV)

And they put away the strange gods from among them, and served the Lord: and his soul was grieved for the misery of Israel.

1 Samuel 30:6 (KJV)

6 And David was greatly distressed; for the people spake of stoning him, because the soul of all the people was grieved, every man for his sons and for his daughters: but David encouraged himself in the Lord his God.

Job 30:25 (KJV)

Did not I weep for him that was in trouble? Was not my soul grieved for the poor?

There is so much more we can say about the soul. When I did a word search for the soul, the results pulled up about 443 times in the bible that the soul was mentioned. That is an indication of how important your soul is to God.

Then the question remains how is this relevant to the counselees that we see for inner healing? It is very simple as counselors we must also act as teachers. We must teach our counselees how to build up their inner man. In fact, although you may be like me and haven't heard a lot of teaching specifically about soul care, you more than likely have heard about building the inner man.

After the counselee has gone through inner healing work, remember we said a lot about how we can't just leave them hanging, we have to give them tools to live by. Teaching the counselee how to build their inner man is vitally important. Remember it is one thing to get delivered it is another thing to stay delivered. Building the inner man is another word for building or restoring the soul.

Before we end this chapter let us look at some final principles of how to build the inner man.

Back to David as our example:

1 Samuel 30:6King James Version (KJV)

6 And David was greatly distressed; for the people spake of stoning him, because the soul of all the people was grieved, every man for his sons and for his daughters: but David encouraged himself in the Lord his God.

I tell my client's all the time there is nothing wrong with talking to yourself; you just have to be conscious about what you are saying to yourself. There is no research that says the more you talk down to yourself, the more you will be motivated to change. You can't talk down to your soul or your inner man, and then expect to change.

This may seem like a menial concept, but as a counselor, I cannot begin to tell you how many clients's will put themselves down. I work with people who have very low confidence. When you have low self-esteem or confidence, you have a very hard time seeing yourself in a positive light. It is almost unheard of to see yourself the way God sees you when you have low confidence.

Notice in the scripture we read David encouraged himself in the Lord. He didn't encourage himself in himself. This again is the difference between Christian mental health counseling and secular mental health counseling. Secular counseling teaches us this Buddhist like concepts where we simply look into ourselves for divine guidance or divine light.

We find ourselves in the word of God. We look to God for divine guidance and divine light. Divine simply means supernatural power.

We then must teach our client's how to meditate on the word of God. Again I am not using the word meditate like the secular world. Remember I keep saying the secular world borrows from the Bible and takes Christ out of it. Meditate means to think deeply or carefully about (something). The act of meditating is to take something that you want your heart and soul to remember, and begin to be repeatedly about putting the word of God in your mouth and heart. In the secular world meditating is again doing like the Buddhist, sitting on your bottom, hands together, and meditating focusing on getting to the inner light. We don't do such a thing, yet scripture tells us to meditate.

Joshua 1:8 (NKJV)

8 This Book of the Law shall not depart from your mouth, but you shall **meditate** in it day and night, that you may observe to do according to all that is written in it. For then you will make your way prosperous, and then you will have good success.

Psalm 1:2 (NKJV)

 But his delight is in the law of the Lord, And in His law he **meditates** day and night.

Psalm 4:4 (NKJV)

 Be angry, and do not sin. **Meditate** within your heart on your bed, and be still. Selah

Psalm 63:6 (NKJV)

When I remember You on my bed, I **meditate on You** in the night watches.

Psalm 77:6 (NKJV)

I call to remembrance my song in the night; I **meditate** within my heart, And my spirit makes a diligent search.

Psalm 77:12 (NKJV)

I will also **meditate** on all Your work, And talk of Your deeds.

Psalm 119:15 (NKJV)

I will **meditate** on Your precepts, And contemplate Your ways.

Psalm 119:23 (NKJV)

Princes also sit and speak against me, But Your servant **meditates** on Your statutes.

Psalm 119:27 (NKJV)

 Make me understand the way of Your precepts; So shall I **meditate** on Your wonderful works.

Psalm 119:48 (NKJV)

My hands also I will lift up to Your commandments, Which I love, And I will **meditate** on Your statutes.

Psalm 119:78 (NKJV)

 Let the proud be ashamed, For they treated me wrongfully with falsehood; But I will **meditate** on Your precepts.

Psalm 119:148 (NKJV)

My eyes are awake through the night watches, That I may **meditate** on Your word.

Psalm 143:5 (KJV)

I remember the days of old; I **meditate** on all Your works; I muse on the work of Your hands.

Psalm 145:5 (KJV)

I will **meditate** on the glorious splendor of Your majesty, And on Your wondrous works.

Isaiah 33:18 (KJV)

Your heart will **meditate** on terror: "Where is the scribe? Where is he who weighs? Where is he who counts the towers?"

Malachi 3:16 (KJV)

 [A Book of Remembrance] Then those who feared the Lord spoke to one another, And the Lord listened and heard them; So a book of remembrance was written before Him For those who fear the Lord And who **meditate** on His name.

Luke 21:14 (KJV)

Therefore settle it in your hearts not to **meditate** beforehand on what you will answer;

Philippians 4:8 (KJV)

[**Meditate** on These Things] Finally, brethren, whatever things are true, whatever things are noble, whatever things are just, whatever things are pure, whatever things are lovely, whatever things are of good report, if there is any virtue and if there is anything praiseworthy—meditate on these things.

1 Timothy 4:15 (KJV)

Meditate on these things; give yourself entirely to them, that your progress may be evident to all.

Meditating in Christ is the intentional and repetitive act of thinking upon the word of God. We are not meditating for meditating sake; we are meditating or discerning the word. Meditating is not a religious act or regimen; it is establishing a relationship with God.

In fact, most Christians meditate, we just don't call it meditating. For example, I went to church yesterday, the word of God was amazing. I listened to the same word after church it was so good. Then on my hour long commute to get to my office today, I listened to the same message the entire way. What was I doing? Meditating. What was I meditating on? The word of God. I was not meditating on my pastor or his style of preaching; I was repeatedly listening to the word of God, he was the vessel being used.

Have you ever did a study on a particular topic and found scriptures related to that? Guess what you were doing meditating. In fact, I have an inner healing client that I am working with now. She suffers from chronic fear that is causing panic attacks. Do you know why? Of course, we can talk about family history, trauma all of the above, but it has more to do about what she is meditating n. The enemy puts fear thoughts in her mind, and she thinks on them repeatedly. Therefore she is meditating on the wrong thing.

So I had to teach her principles about fear, I hand her my book called *No Fear*. Then I hand her scriptures about fear for her to begin to read. I told her in the morning take one scripture and say it repeatedly in the morning and then again at night. I don't want her meditating to be a religious act, but an act of relationship. The more word she gets in her, the more she is building her inner man. She has to meditate on the word of God.

No, she doesn't have to sit on the floor, with her eyes closed and her hands together. All meditating on is taking a scripture or scriptures and implanting them into herself, so her soul will begin to mend.

You have to be careful what you think on.

Have you ever had your favorite song you loved so much that you kept it on repeat? This past week I have been listening to a song sung by Miranda Curtis, Let Praises Rise. I have worn that song out it has been on repeat. Guess what I was doing? Meditating.

What I tell my client's is to pick a mantra song and play it over and over again, until you feel it has gotten in your spirit. This is biblical.

Psalm 77:6 (NKJV)

I call to remembrance my song in the night; I **meditate** within my heart, And my spirit makes diligent search.

We have to teach our inner healing counselee's to do what they already do but be intentional about it. Just as it works in the positive, it works for the negative. If I played some sad song in my spirit, it would start making me depressed I don't care how beautiful the song is. I know what it cost for me to maintain my soul so I don't listen to music, movies or anything that will replay in my mind. I can't watch reality television shows because I will get depressed and start counseling these ladies in my dreams.

We have to teach our client's to be intentional about their own inner healing. I had a psychiatrist I worked with who said that when it comes to his client's he would not work harder than they would.

I agree I will not work harder for my client's than they are willing to work for themselves.

Finally, we have to teach our client's to begin to declare the word of God over themselves. We have to teach them to begin to speak the word of God. We already read in several verses how David began to speak to his soul. If David can do it so can we. Let us look at some final examples. Attached is a sample decree. A decree is something that someone can declare or speak over their lives.

Decree

Soul, you shall live and not die

Soul, you shall be in Christ.

I break the spirit of depression in you soul.

In the name of Jesus soul, you are healed.

I declare Holy Spirit power in my mind, heart, and soul.

Soul, you shall not lead the way, Holy Spirit you lead.

Hopefully, you get the examples. Remember you can think yourself so much that you get sad, or you can think yourself so much you get happy. Let your soul be in Christ.

Acts 26:2 (KJV)

2 **I think myself happy**, king Agrippa, because I shall answer for myself this day before thee touching all the things whereof I am accused of the Jews:

Apostle Paul was in a situation where his soul could have been discouraged. He was in court, yet his perception changed, he looked at what could have been devastating and saw the opportunity in it.

Psalm 23:3 (KJV)

He restoreth my soul: he leadeth me in the paths of righteousness for his name's sake.

Lastly, let us look at the formula as found in the Word of God.

Psalm 1(NKJV)

Psalms 1—6

The Way of the Righteous and the End of the Ungodly

1 Blessed is the man

Who walks not in the counsel of the ungodly,

    Nor stands in the path of sinners,

    Nor sits in the seat of the scornful;

2 But his delight is in the law of the Lord,

    And in His law he meditates day and night.

3 He shall be like a tree

    Planted by the rivers of water,

    That brings forth its fruit in its season,

    Whose leaf also shall not wither;

And whatever he does shall prosper.

4 The ungodly are not so,

But are like the chaff which the wind drives away.

5 Therefore the ungodly shall not stand in the judgment,

Nor sinners in the congregation of the righteous.

6 For the Lord knows the way of the righteous,

But the way of the ungodly shall perish.

And the formula is:

***Seek Godly counsel** (for us as counselors in our own personal lives and in our counselees, are you giving them godly counsel? Are you receiving godly counseling?) As stated I am a licensed mental health counselor and have learned all kinds of strategies and theories for counseling clients, that doesn't mean I use all them. I only give my client's godly biblical counsel. So I use strategies that line up with the word of God. If the strategies do not line up with the word of God, I don't use them.

***Delight** (take pleasure in the Lord) When a person loves God they will be drawn to Him and be open to His principles. It is hard to counsel someone in inner healing work when their heart is secretly against godly principles. This happens when you have a counselee that says they are a Christian or they God, but in talking with them, you start sensing something else in their spirit. Use discernment.

***When I delight myself in the Lord, He stabilizes my heart and mind. I become planted, not double minded, but secure.**

James 1:8 (KJV)

8 A double minded man is unstable in all his ways

Seek God first.

Chapter 9

Healing Trauma Through Christ

2 Timothy 1:7 (KJV)

7 For God hath not given us the spirit of fear; but of power, and of love, and of a sound mind.

We first must understand that the mission of Jesus Christ was to first and foremost heal, set free and deliver. My focus within my counseling practice is to work with individuals who are trying to overcome early childhood sexual abuse. I know firsthand how the wounds of sexual abuse and impact a person for a lifetime. It is my opinion that the ONLY answer to healing the trauma of abuse is the healing power of Jesus. In my experience working with this population absent from Christ in the secular arena a person gets to the place where they can function, but they never fully recover, depending on the severity of the trauma. When I studied how to work with this population I found the answers in the Word of God. Complete healing and wholeness are found in Christ Jesus.

Isaiah 61:1(KJV)

61 …………. because the Lord hath anointed me to preach good tidings unto the meek; he hath sent me to bind up the brokenhearted, to proclaim liberty to the captives, and the opening of the prison to them that are bound;

As stated before the scripture Isaiah was the mission of Jesus it was one of the primary reasons He was sent. We assume in the body of Christ that Jesus main focus was to physically heal, and it was, but if you look at the text very carefully, Jesus was sent to heal individual wounds as well. You can't see a broken heart, it is invisible but very much there. Jesus wasn't just referring to people in physical prisons when he said captives. The text also meant people that have invisible wounds and invisible prisons and are held captive in their minds.

The pointers that I will give you are in no particular order, and this is not an all-inclusive list.

1. Break the power of the soul tie/soul connection.

We talked about speaking to your soul in a previous chapter. Soul connections are dangerous. I was asked at a conference I was teaching at why people in domestic violence relationships have such difficulty leaving. The reality is because there is a soul connection. A soul tie is a demonic spiritual connection between two people.

This is why a woman can beat up but won't leave that relationship or vice versa.

You can also have a soul connection to a dead person. I know sounds strange right.

I have a client that I was working with for a couple of years. He was raised in a very violent home where he was severely beaten by his parents. His parents had since deceased over 15 years ago. He is a man in his 50's; he still is afraid of being beaten up or hurt. Remember I said his parents have been deceased for many years. Why? Even though he experienced devastating trauma, there is a soul connection there. Remember people die spirits do not. The same power, control, and rage that his parents inflicted on him, is still there.

We need to do to break the power of soul connects and pray that God would give us a new heart.

Ezekiel 11:19-20 (KJV)

19 And I will give them one heart, and I will put a new spirit within you; and I will take the stony heart out of their flesh, and will give them an heart of flesh:

20 That they may walk in my statutes, and keep mine ordinances, and do them: and they shall be my people, and I will be their God.

God promises to give us a new heart. When a person has experienced severe trauma in their lives, their heart is full of fear. Thanks be to God there is an answer found in Christ Jesus.

Another principle that we discussed is that we must teach our counselees is forgiveness even when there have been traumas. A person cannot heal when forgiveness is not present. We won't go into detail about this because we have already studied a great deal about forgiveness in a previous chapter, however, lets review several powerful stories about forgiveness.

Officer Van de Broek, tortured, killed the husband of a South African woman and their child during Apartheid. The officer admitted to the crimes that included shooting her son, burning his body and then holding a party nearby.

At the court hearing, the judge asked the woman how justice should be rendered. She responded by requesting that the officer visit her twice a month so she could be a mother to him and share her love. She then hugs him so that he could know that he is forgiven and to show the love of Jesus.

Often we find it difficult to forgive because of the emotional damage that took place as a result of the offense or the person who committed the wrong act. Think about it, the people that love us the most are the people who can hurt us the most.

When a person has mother or father wounds they can run deep, they can find it very difficult to forgive. Most people don't carry the heavy wounds of unforgiveness over someone who has no relevance or position in their lives. In the case of the South African woman, it would have been very easy for her to hold unforgiveness due to the crime and severe loss.

South African Woman Forgives Murderer's Son (n.d). Retrieved July 1, 2015, http://www.geoffsshorts.blogspot.com

In the book Let It Go author Chris Williams talks about his story of tragedy to forgiveness. On February 2007 his wife, unborn baby, nine year old daughter and eleven year old son were all killed by a drunk driver. Mr. Williams decided to forgive.

On February 1993, Mrs. Margaret Johnson's only son, Laramiun Byrd, 20 was murdered by a then 16 year old Israel. The 16 year old was charged as an adult and sentenced to 25 years in prison. He ended up spending 17 years in prison. Mrs. Johnson originally reported that she hated him and had no desire to forgive. Eventually, it was her faith and facilitating a support group that led her to forgive. A few years ago she began to meet regularly with her son's murderer Israel at Minnesota's Stillwater state prison.

Eventually, after his release from prison, she helped him get an apartment in her apartment complex. Ironically they are now neighbors. He lives right next to her. They are now close friends. She is quoted by saying, "'Unforgiveness is like cancer. It will eat you from the inside out." She is also quoted saying, "forgiveness does not diminish what he did, but forgiveness is for me."

Woman Shows Incredible Mercy. (2011, June 8) Retrieved July 3, 2015, from ww.dailymail.co.uk.new/article-incredible-mercy-sons-killer-movies-door.htm.

I used these examples because it gives us illustrations of people who experienced extreme trauma and forgave. I have heard some people say that there are somethings that I could never forgive. My responses are you are right. This kind of forgiveness only comes from a supernatural place. This forgiveness is only found through the Holy Spirit.

For the most part, the inner healing counselor must address fear in the counselee. The trauma is gone, but the fear associated with the trauma more than likely will be ever present.

Other basic tips when doing inner healing with this population is that you have to be careful in inner healing, some of the individuals you meet with will be very vulnerable and fragile. This is where you may have to teach them self-management healing skills before you dive into the trauma. If an individual is not comfortable talking about the trauma, it doesn't mean that you can't counsel them. The disclosure is not as important as the healing.

For example, I have an inner healing client that I work with on a regular basis who doesn't remember anything about her trauma. Her mind blocked it out. She meets all the criteria verbatim for post trauma stress disorder. She remembers glimpse only not full detail. Because her conscious mind doesn't remember doesn't mean she can't be healed. Ironically most of our therapy sessions are about the fear.

If you are not a mental health counselor and feel overwhelmed you have to know when to refer to a mental health counselor. Watch your facial expressions. Some of the stories I have heard are downright deplorable. I have heard stories of women who remember details about them being sexually abused as five and six year old children. My most recent client was made to perform oral sex on an individual. I had another client that told me how she was made to perform oral sex at the age of four on an adult male.

My point is these stories are not for the faint at heart. It is not for someone who doesn't have the heart to meet with individuals who have experienced sexual abuse. You may have individuals who struggle with their sexual identity as a result of the sexual abuse they suffered.

I had other client who was sexually assaulted by a grown man beginning at the age of 3. After repeated sexual assaults, through her childhood, adolescents, she became a lesbian. She would tell me she knew it was wrong how she felt but couldn't see herself with a man because of what she had been through.

I know that homosexual lifestyles are not of God. Yet and still if a person cannot be honest and transparent before someone who is supposed to represent Christ, where else can they go to get healed? Yes we know it is wrong, but this is not the time to minister to the counselee about how wrong their lifestyle is. Just because you are counseling someone whose lifestyle is not of God doesn't mean you agree.

Remember the onion that we talked about at the beginning of the book. You can deal with the symptoms or you can deal with the root. Effective inner healing although we are aware of the symptoms, we deal with the root, then the Lord heals, which will eventually eliminate the symptoms. Homosexually, lesbians, transgender issues are symptoms that suggest something in the root that has to be dealt with.

As you minister to Christ, He will begin to transform the counselee. We offer them the word; it is the word that begins to transform.

Finally be authentic, be real, show kindness. When a person who has been gone through any abuse particularly sexual abuse, they will often feel a sense of shame, guilt. We **NEVER** blame the victim. We minister Christ to them. The same strategies that we discussed before will need to be used here. Use the prophetic and the word of knowledge in particular because sometimes a person tells you what they think they want you to hear and not the truth in order to get unstuck we need the Holy Spirit will reveal the truth.

Another thing to consider when dealing with trauma is married couples. If a person was raised in a violent domestic home or a home where they were sexually abused it will impact their marriage. An individual may have problems being sexually intimate with their spouse. They may have issues trusting their spouse or showing love to their children. This is significant because trauma survivors have been taught the wrong kind of love.

For some, they have been taught that how they use their bodies equates to love. For others being hit is how thy equate to love. So you have to again act as the teacher, share the scriptures about love, the principles of love, and invite the Holy Spirit into the session to show them about love. You may start with I Corinthians 13

1 Corinthians 13:4-7 (NKJV)

4 Love suffers long and is kind; love does not envy; love does not parade itself, is not puffed up;

5 does not behave rudely, does not seek its own, is not provoked, thinks no evil;

6 does not rejoice in iniquity, but rejoices in the truth;

7 bears all things, believes all things, hopes all things, endures all things.

Ask the couples or the individual to compare the principles of love found in the scripture to the love they experienced growing up. What was similar about it? What was different?

This is where you have to be the master surgeon and begin to by the Holy Spirit take out the poison in their hearts by using the word and then input perfect love by the sword of the spirit which is the word.

Hopefully, you can tell that the inner healing counselor is not just a counselor but a teacher as well. So many of our counselees may have never been taught to value themselves, their bodies, how to honor themselves and their spouses. It is not common knowledge. You literarily have to teach biblical principles.

By the way, I do not counsel couples where they are actively engaged in domestic violence or sexual abuse. It is a liability for me. Also when one partner is intimidating the other, the session is not going to be authentic.

I have counseled women that are in domestic violence relationships but not couples. Be careful what you say. Other things to consider when counseling domestic violence counselees are the security of the building believe it or not. I am the only one who has access to my building; you can't just walk up on off the streets and request an appointment. This is important because if you are dealing with someone who has a stalker, or who has just left a violent relationship, the more secure you are, and they are the better.

I had a client that I counseled in one of my other offices. One day he showed up when the building was closed I just so happened to be in the building. I played it cooled, but my feelings of danger went up. This individual had a very bad past, had been in prison although I never had any problems out of him it gave me red flags to be alone with him.

This same individual would end of up doing things like sit in his car and wait for me to leave. Then he would show up at random places where I was after he knew what my car looked like. It turns out he was on the run from federal probation. So the police and his probation offer where looking for him, and couldn't find him, yet he would show up at random places where I was. What made me extremely comfortable was when in our counseling sessions he started flirting with me, asking me about my personal life. After I would not budge and he didn't understand my explanation of professional boundaries I was done with him.

My point is you have to understand professional boundaries. This may be different from church counselors, because you may counsel with someone then go out to eat with them or be friends. I caution you against this. In my work we cannot have dual relationships, it is considered a conflict of interest. We as counselors must set professional boundaries. Although I tend to counsel with women, I also counsel with men as well. I tend to counsel more with women because we typically see more disclosures of sexual trauma from women.

As a business woman, an entrepreneur I am perfectly fine meeting with both men and women. However I must maintain professional and personal boundaries. I am not friends with my counselees. I am not Facebook friends with my counselees. The lines of interpersonal communications and relationships are very clear. Again these boundaries may not be as clear outside of the traditional human services practices. Particularly in traditional ministry, the boundaries may not be as clear. You always want to set boundaries when you first meet with a counselee. Some counselors have the counselee fill out a professional disclosure form.

I don't counsel people in my home, although I do have a home office. My office is separate. My counselees don't have my cell phone number. I do not accept gifts. The only money that I will accept is if they are paying for services rendered. I don't accept monetary gifts for myself. Because I work with individuals who some have no insurance if an individuals wants to gift extra counseling sessions to someone they are more than welcome to do so. Again document, document and document, your interactions with the counselee. Even if they call to cancel their appointment, I document a non billable note. If I have a discharge someone, I send them a ten day letter that they are pending discharge, in ten days I discharge.

Again you do not have to meet with someone who is making you feel uncomfortable. You should for your liability document your concerns, before discharge. Remember if it is not documented it didn't happen.

I also am required to have liability insurance that covers me and my practice.

 Of course, I cannot and do not disclose any information to outside people. This is common knowledge in the counseling arena, however things you may want to emphasize when initiating counseling sessions with the client. Make sure you let them know limitations, for example if a person discloses of a plan to harm themselves or another you have to break the safety agreement. Even if you are counseling married couples get both of them to complete the individual paperwork, with consents for each other.

I recently read of a counselor who was doing marriage counseling for a couple that was considering going through a divorce. When they initially came in they came to save the marriage, so only one filled out the paperwork, demographic form, etc. It was mutually agreed that they would seek counseling together. They ended up still going through a divorce; the counselor ended up continuing to treat one person. To make a long story short, the counselor ended up getting sued because he released information to the courts regarding the spouse when it was not documented, no disclosure forms or treatment plans. The counselor was found to be in violation of the HIPPA laws. Even though they came in together initially, there was only treatment documentation for one not the other and no written agreement to release information.

Remember confidentially, and HIPPA laws apply even in Christian private practice.

 In fact, I had to act as a mandated reporter for a child I was counseling who disclosed abuse. All these limitations are stated upfront BEFORE the counseling sessions begin.

Another reason why I don't counsel individuals over the phone or skype. If I have to call in reinforcements or get extra help, I don't have as much at my disposal if I am counseling you over the phone and you can just hang up over skype. I have had individuals who disclose of suicidal thoughts. If the individual is severe enough, I have to intervene. I am limited to how much I can intervene if you are in a different state and I am talking to you over electronic media. Also confidentially is not guaranteed and limited when you are gathering information over electronic devices. I am very careful what I put in my case note in the case my records are subpoenaed.

I do not speak or make judgements on custody issues. If any of this makes you uncomfortable, refer out, refer out, refer out if you are an inner healing counselor in private practice you can choose what client's you see and don't see. If there is something beyond your cope of practice that is okay, it doesn't make you a bad person it just means that is not your area. There is someone that can better serve the client.

In fact as a part of my licensure we ethically cannot practice beyond our scope of practice. Mean we cannot counsel someone when we are not knowledgeable about how to treat their diagnosis do not know their particular issues

For example, I cannot treat autism spectrum the most, I can do is to pray for your child as a God fearing

Christian. I cannot offer treatment. I can't charge you for treatment either.

There are many ethical concerns that we must consider when doing this type of work.

Chapter 10

Do you really trust God? A manifestation of anxiety and depression.

Philippians 4:6 (NKJV)

6 Be anxious for nothing, but in everything by prayer and supplication, with thanksgiving, let your requests be made known to God;

Anxiety is a feeling of worry, nervousness, or unease, typically about an imminent event or something with an uncertain outcome. We know what anxiety is but look again at the characteristics that define anxiety again. Worry is to allow one's mind to dwell on difficulty or troubles. It means you constantly think about something bad that has happened or could happen. Nervousness is the state of being easily agitated, alarmed, high strung. Uncertainty is not able to rely on, not trusting, non-confident, it means to doubt. I know this may appear menial, but we are going somewhere I promise.

Depression is a spirit of heaviness. Depression means feeling sad, hopelessness, feeling unimportant, without purpose.

Now let us look at the fruit of the spirit.

Galatians 5:22-23 (NKJV)

22 But the fruit of the Spirit is love, joy, peace, longsuffering, kindness, goodness, faithfulness,

23 gentleness, self-control. Against such, there is no law.

It is ironic that the characteristics of the fruit of the spirit are the complete opposite of characteristics of depression and anxiety.

The reality is when a person is full of anxiety they do not trust God. Why? Because anxiety is worry that what we don't we don't want to happen will happen. We secretly don't believe that God is going to take care of us, so we become anxious. Anxiety doesn't have to be something about big, but it can be.

Recently I was in a situation where I had a bill due that I didn't know where the money was going to come from. My basic needs were met, but this bill was much too big for me. Yes even as a counselor I have to live the same thing I teach. So there I was so anxious to the point of feeling physically sick, I couldn't eat, barely slept. This went on for weeks. I had to keep applying the word of God to my heart, yet the other side of my mind just kept saying over and over again, "what am I going to do? What am I going to do?" No matter how I worked the numbers, I just couldn't find a way. Another thing that causes anxiety is when we are trying to find our way, instead of believing God to do it.

I am not saying we do nothing, but when your back is against the wall, and you don't have a clue what direction to take, we have to know in our inner man it is God who takes care of us. I confess it is easier said than done. In this situation, I couldn't call anyone for help. I didn't have the resources, all I had was God. But again I was full of anxiety because I didn't see how God was going to move on my behave and I also secretly was afraid that He wouldn't do it.

I am transparent here because I believe we all can relate. The truth of the matter is no matter me being a Christian, a counselor, teaching these things I didn't trust God like I said I did. When I came to this conclusion, it was a hard pill to swallow. I am not saying I am perfect, but for me to have a heart to heart with myself and realize that in all that I had accomplished I didn't trust God, I cried for myself. To me, miss super saint doesn't trust God like she said she does was a humbling experience. I had to look at the one I said I love and admit to Him that I was having a hard time trusting Him as much as I loved Him.

The reality is that God knew it. The circumstance I was going through was not meant to hurt me. I realized that it was God. He knows what is in our hearts before we do. He was using the circumstance to develop me and to teach me to trust Him. After it was all said and done, what I had been physically sick over for weeks, and anxious God resolved in less than five minutes. Again it was God developing me. It was a test only a test. My point in sharing this is, so I don't come across as some arrogant counselor. When I say you are full of anxiety because you don't trust God, I am not saying that from a place of condemnation. I have been there; I went through the test. In fact, if I am honest there have been many, many tests in this area. God told me this same thing repeatedly about myself. We have to be able to use wisdom when confronting our clients with the word of God.

Ask them what they are anxious about? Whatever it is no matter the different circumstance it boils down to not trusting God. We don't believe that He is going to do it. We don't believe the scripture about Him being our protector, so we think something bad is going to happen. When fear is present faith is absent. You can't feel God's presence when your full of anxiety. He seems so far away.

Before we move forward, there are two main scriptures that God gave me to deal with anxiety. I encourage you to have them printed out. When meeting with the counselee, you can read over them together. Remember we talked about meditating on the scripture in a previous chapter these two scripture must be mainstays in your arsenal of biblical wellness tools. Let's read them together.

Matthew 6:25-34 (NKJV)

Do Not Worry

25 "Therefore I say to you, **do not worry about your life**, what you will eat or what you will drink; nor about your body, what you will put on. Is not life more than food and the body more than clothing?

26 Look at the birds of the air, for they neither sow nor reap nor gather into barns; yet your heavenly Father feeds them. Are you not of more value than they?

27 **Which of you by worrying can add one cubit to his stature?**

28 "**So why do you worry about clothing**? Consider the lilies of the field, how they grow: they neither toil nor spin;

29 and yet I say to you that even Solomon in all his glory was not arrayed like one of these.

30 Now if God so clothes the grass of the field, which today is, and tomorrow is thrown into the oven, will He not much more clothe you, O you of little faith?

31 "**Therefore do not worry, saying,** 'What shall we eat?' or 'What shall we drink?' or 'What shall we wear?'

32 For after all these things the Gentiles seek. For your heavenly Father knows that you need all these things.

33 But seek first the kingdom of God and His righteousness, and all these things shall be added to you.

34 **Therefore do not worry about tomorrow, for tomorrow will worry about its own things.** Sufficient for the day is its own trouble.

The text above is a promise from God. It mentions do not worry six times in the text. God says that when we worry we have little faith. I would assume when you worry you have no faith, but Jesus said, "little faith." That means when we worry it is not that we don't have faith, we have faith in the wrong directions.

Let me explain God faith brings us closer to the promises of God. We believe that God is going to do what He said even though we don't have any physical evidence to prove what He said.

Hebrews 11:1 (NKJV)

11 Now faith is the substance of things hoped for, the evidence of things not seen.

What is fear? Fear is what takes us away from the promises of God. Fear is faith in the opposite direction. It is the belief or feeling of uncertainty that what we don't want to happen, will happen although we have no physical evidence to prove it. It is a demonic faith.

You can't trust God and be anxious at the same time. Now the other scripture, this one is great for those who have ever experienced any trauma (natural disasters, physical abuse, rape, etc.). Often trauma survivors subconsciously believe that something else bad will happen.

Psalm 91 (NKJV)

91 He who dwells in the secret place of the highest

Shall abide under the shadow of the Almighty.

2 I will say of the Lord, "He is my refuge and my fortress;

My God, in Him I will trust."

3 Surely He shall deliver you from the snare of the fowler[a]

And from the perilous pestilence.

4 He shall cover you with His feathers,

And under His wings you shall take refuge;

His truth shall be your shield and buckler.

5 You shall not be afraid of the terror by night,

Nor of the arrow that flies by day,

6 Nor of the pestilence that walks in darkness,

Nor of the destruction that lays waste at noonday.

7 A thousand may fall at your side,

And ten thousand at your right hand;

But it shall not come near you.

8 Only with your eyes shall you look,

And see the reward of the wicked.

9 Because you have made the Lord, who is my refuge,

Even the Most High, your dwelling place,

10 No evil shall befall you,

Nor shall any plague come near your dwelling;

11 For He shall give His angels charge over you,

To keep you in all your ways.

12 In their hands they shall bear you up,

Lest you dash your foot against a stone.

13 You shall tread upon the lion and the cobra,

The young lion and the serpent you shall trample underfoot.

14 "Because he has set his love upon Me, therefore I will deliver him;

I will set him on high, because he has known My name.

15 He shall call upon Me, and I will answer him;

I will be with him in trouble;

I will deliver him and honor him.

16 With long life I will satisfy him,

And show him My salvation.

Make sure as you are going over this scripture with a counselee you don't gloss over anything. Have them read it in detail. For those who bring their bible to session have them read it in their bible. This is very powerful. Remember we said what we said about meditating on the word of God, this is one scripture that must seep deep into their psyche. Psyche (spirit, soul, mind)

What about depression? One of the main symptoms of depression is hopeless. When a person experiences depression, they have lost hope and faith. Maybe they believed God for something that didn't happen. Maybe they had so many down days that they don't believe that things will get better. The other side of depression is when a person is stuck in the past. Their minds replay what happened to them in the past, to the point where they can't see a brighter future. A person cannot truly trust God and be depressed at the same time. We need to rely on the Holy Spirit.

Teach your counselees how to have an authentic relationship with the Holy Spirit. Remember you can't teach what you don't know. Your success as a counselor has a lot to do with how you have been prepared and processed in secret. In fact something I posted on Facebook the other day.

You can be the most gifted singer, writer, preacher whatever it is only experience, hardships and struggles that create something beautiful. The oil of the anointing is created through the pressures of life not the ease of life.

It is here where we use scripture to input hope back into the counselee. You start by encouraging words. Have the counselee talk about time they overcame a tragedy or something that happened to them that they were able to make it through then, point out to them that they came out before and they will do it again.

It is the same with someone who has anxiety; you have them talk about a time when they were worried about something that they overcame in the past. This is what we counselors call suggestive reasoning. Another name of it is socratic questioning. It means you ask the counselee a question in such a way, that it makes them think and then rethink. Let's look at an example.

Counselor "so you are telling me that when your grandmother passed away, you had no hope and thought, you would never make it out? Is that correct?"

Counselee "Yes."

Counselee "But in this situation, you are telling me because you are going through a divorce you think there is no hope and you will never make it out is that correct?"

Counselee "Yes but I……"

Counselor "so tell me again if you made it through that other devastation, how is it you won't make it through this one?"

This just a suggestion. Are you seeing that the counselor is not giving the counselor the answers, the counselor is using suggestive questions that get the counselee to think? It would help if you had the counselee to talk about more than one experience.

Also again use scriptures, then use the suggestive reasoning to confront wrong mindsets. Let review another example. Say you have a counselee who is struggling with a broken heart, maybe they feel that God has abandoned them. You then pull out a scripture that speaks to their situation.

Psalm 34:18-19 (NKJV)

18 The Lord is near to those who have a broken heart,

And saves such as have a contrite spirit.

19 Many are the afflictions of the righteous,

But the Lord delivers him out of them all.

So you read the scripture together or have the counselee read the scripture.

Counselor "so tell me what do you think this scripture is saying?"

Counselee "it is saying that God is near to the broken hearted."

Counselor "but you are telling me due to this relationship ending you had prayed about it and believe that God has abandoned you is that correct?"

Counselee "yes but….."

Counselor "so I just want to know who you think is not telling the truth is it the Bible? Or can their be another answer?"

Do you see the technique? Again this should not come across as mean or judgmental. You can't get the tone I am coming from because you are reading my words not hearing them. If done correctly it shouldn't come off as condescending but loving. We all must confront our thoughts about life and God to see how it holds up to the word of God.

My hope is that you see that the counselor is not just giving the answer but is using suggestive reasoning in such a way that gets the counselor to rethink what they think is the truth.

By the way, you must know the word of God to use this technique. You the counselor do not have to agree with everything the counselee says. You are there being used as an agent of the most high God to bring them out.

Remember depression is a spirit that can be lifted off of anyone. As stated there are some deliverances that happened overnight but then there are some that happen overtime and in process. It is my opinion that deliverance from the stronghold of depression and anxiety happen overtime and in process.

Chapter 11

When to conduct Deliverance Ministry in the counseling session?

Luke 8:30 (KJV)

30 And Jesus asked him, saying, What is thy name? And he said, Legion: because many devils were entered into him

We cannot fully discuss the aspects of inner healing without talking about deliverance ministry. When we use the term deliverance ministry in the modern day vernacular, we are referring to casting out of demons.

Every person that comes to you for mental health counseling or inner healing counseling is not being influenced by a demon. This is a common myth within the body of Christ and reason why many people don't seek out counseling. It is a big myth that when Christians present with mental health conditions, they are demon possessed and just need someone to lay hands on them to make them better.

Again this is a common myth. Every mental health condition is not the manifestation of a demon.

However even with all of the myths, we cannot deny that demons do exist, and they need to be cast out of people. As inner healing counselors, you may be the first one someone calls. They initially may not tell you that they have a demon or they may not know it, yet they are there.

You have to know when this is not a standard counseling session and deliverance ministry is needed. This chapter will not give you all the information you need about deliverance ministry but rather how to discern when a demon is present.

Another myth within Christendom that many believe that if a person is a Christian they cannot have demons, that is a myth. A Christian can be influenced by a demon. Let me explained, possessed means possession it simply means ownership. Possession also means control, hands, keeping, care, custody, charge, hold, title, guardianship. When you profess Christ, you are no longer owned by the devil or his demons because God owns you.

You can be oppressed by the demonic. Oppression and possession are two different things, which is why

I believe many Christians are confused about the two. Oppression means persecution, abuse, maltreatment, ill-treatment, tyranny, despotism, repression, suppression, subjection, subjugation. Another word for oppression is an influence.

A Christian can be influenced or oppressed by a demon. There will be a time when you the inner healing counselor will meet with a counselee who is either oppressed by a demon or possessed by a demon. What I experience more so than possession is individuals who are oppressed by a demon.

Let me give you an example. I have a client who is a Christian. He reads his bible and prays, loves Jesus.

The demons talk to him, put him down, tell him he is nothing. This individual has a long history of trauma. In the session I prayed with him, I taught him about Jesus Christ that lives in Him and His power over the enemy. Still nothing, He comes to sessions, but the demons don't budge. I had to lean on the Holy Spirit, asking Him why won't the demonic leave this man's life when he prays, reads the bible, I prayed with him. The Holy Spirit let me know due to unforgiveness. You see there are certain instances where the demonic has legal right to oppress someone even a Christian.

This individual has gone through so much as a child. When I tried to teach him about how forgiveness can heal his heart, he says he knows he needs to forgive, but he can't do it right now. He keeps replaying the trauma over and over again in his head. When the demons speak to him they add to the trauma by telling him that he is stupid, he should end it all, etc. Which by the way he is committed not to listen to the voices, otherwise known as demons.

That puts us in a stuck place because since he refuses to forgive, the demons have legal right to be there. There are some instances where a demon won't leave even when it is cast out, and one of them is when unforgiveness is present.

So what do I do as a inner healing counselor? I don't discharge him from my practice because he won't forgive. Even though we are at a stuck place. We just have sessions about forgiveness. That leads me to a point maybe you have a person that is like my client won't forgive, that doesn't mean you don't meet with them anymore. Remember a great deal of our practice is learning and teaching individuals the process of transformation. I fully believe he will get there.

This is an instance where you can still minister to the person, even with the demons present. I have heard it said many times that you couldn't counsel a demon and that is true, but you can the person. You have to use discernment in these cases.

Demons recognize the authority that you walk in. I still take authority over the atmosphere; the demons are quiet long enough for me to plant the seeds that I need to. When he attends church, the demons are quiet as well per his report. Again that gives him time to hear the word of God. This will eventually prick his heart and lead him to forgive.

There are times when a demon is so disruptive you may have to take authority over the demonic. Again use wisdom.

It can be frightful to think that you the counselor will have to deal with someone who is influenced by a demon, but you have to know that God has equipped you to do what He has called you to do. Inner healing work is not for the novice or the faint of heart.

The first you must be confident in is the authority that God has given you. We said at the very beginning that the inner healing minister is a valid ministry that you must be called and appointed to, God never sends a minister out to do any ministry without first giving them what they need to accomplish the task.

Luke 9:1-2 (NKJV)

9 Then He called His twelve disciples together and gave them power and authority over all demons, and to cure diseases.

2 He sent them to preach the kingdom of God and to heal the sick.

Remember if you have been called and chosen by God you have authority over demons and devils. Be wise about how and when you cast out demons. If you are counseling someone alone and there is not someone in the office with you, use wisdom. Consider team ministry, maybe have a ministry partner. If you feel comfortable or don't have much experience with the demonic use wisdom.

You don't have to have a ministers license to cast out a demon, all you need is to believe.

Mark 16:17-20King James Version (KJV)

17 And these signs shall follow them that believe; In my name shall they cast out devils; they shall speak with new tongues;

18 They shall take up serpents; and if they drink any deadly thing, it shall not hurt them; they shall lay hands on the sick, and they shall recover.

19 So then after the Lord had spoken unto them, he was received up into heaven, and sat on the right hand of God.

20 And they went forth, and preached everywhere, the Lord working with them, and confirming the word with signs following. Amen.

Again the only requirement is believing. Don't send yourselves out into this kind of ministry make sure God has sent you out.

Other things to consider, do not attempt to cast out a demon if the person's lifestyle is sketchy. The demon can be cast out in most cases, (except some principles we talked about) but if the person is not willing to denounce or walk away from a lifestyle that is not of God the demonic will come seven times harder.

Matthew 12:43-47 (NKJV)

43 "When an unclean spirit goes out of a man, he goes through dry places, seeking rest, and finds none.

44 Then he says, 'I will return to my house from which I came.' And when he comes, he finds it empty, swept, and put in order.

45 Then he goes and takes with him seven other spirits more wicked than himself, and they enter and dwell there, and the last state of that man is worse than the first. So shall it also be with this wicked generation."

The scripture is indicating of what happens when a demon is cast out of a person. Notice the scripture doesn't call it a demon it calls it an unclean spirit, which means that you may have to cast out a demon, an unclean spirit or both. Notice the unclean spirit claimed the man's body as his own house. Remember unclean spirits have minds, will, emotions and hidden agendas. Notice the unclean spirit said to himself, "I will go back to my house." It didn't matter that the man had been set free and delivered. How do we know that the unclean spirit was set free and delivered? Because when the unclean spirit came back, he found it clean. This means just because a person gets free doesn't mean they will stay free.

I had a client that I was assigned to when I worked in an inpatient mental health hospital. She identified herself as a voodoo priestess, yet she also complained about being possessed by demons. That sounds like a contradiction within itself. The head psychiatrist was open to spirituality and was looking for a clergy that would agree to cast out a demon. No, I didn't volunteer. Why? It is obvious because she was not willing to let go or denounce of the voodoo lifestyle or priesthood that she was a part of. Voodoo is based upon a demonic religion; she was also not willing to accept Christ. There was no way that casting out the demons would work on this woman.

Be very careful about casting out a demon if someone is not willing to do what we therapist call maintenance therapy. It means you are working with the individual by teaching them tools and strategies to maintain their deliverance. They should also be committed to the church, being in your office once a week doesn't take the place of a good church where God dwells. Let's go back to the scripture, notice the unclean spirit had a strategy.

He said he would bring seven of his friends why? Because unclean spirits don't want to leave willingly and they don't want to stay gone.

My point is the reason we do follow up appointments is that we have to teach the counselee how to maintain their deliverance. It is like building a house, you have set the foundation, you have the walls built, but you must use the sealant to make something airtight or watertight. The aftercare of deliverance is the sealant; it is the guiding principles we use to make sure that the deliverance is airtight and watertight.

If deliverance is not set on a firm foundation, the person is at risk of returning to what they have been previously delivered from. For further clarification, you may want to read my book entitled: *Who Beguiled You?*

Depending on the client you have to teach them skills such as warfare prayers, how to not become prey to the enemy, how to identify false beliefs and patterns, how to identify unhealthy habits and not go back to them. That is what the aftercare is. Doing deliverance work with no follow up care for the inner healing counselor is dangerous for the counselee. I am not talking about your traditional church minister who is ministering at church. Hopefully, the minister gives some aftercare instructions, or give them some direction to allow the church to follow up with the individual.

You contract with the counselee in regards to what type of follow up care. Even if they don't see you after the fact, give them instructions, that includes a list of churches that have a good deliverance ministry. Some people go to a church where God doesn't show up. Of course, don't talk about their church but give them resources. I tell my client's about other churches in the area that have small groups. Give them resources such as books to read. I have given out books to my client's it doesn't just have to be my books. The Purpose Driven Life is a good book to give out. Also the chapters are good for small groups and individual session. Have a list of resources and places the can go.

Another time you should not do deliverance ministry is if you are not clear about your own relationship with God. If you are living in some kind of sin.

Acts 19:11-20 (ESV)

11 And God was doing extraordinary miracles by the hands of Paul,

12 so that even handkerchiefs or aprons that had touched his skin were carried away to the sick, and their diseases left them and the evil spirits came out of them.

13 Then some of the itinerant Jewish exorcists undertook to invoke the name of the Lord Jesus over those who had evil spirits, saying, "I adjure you by the Jesus whom Paul proclaims."

14 Seven sons of a Jewish high priest named Sceva were doing this.

15 But the evil spirit answered them, "Jesus I know, and Paul I recognize, but who are you?"

16 And the man in whom was the evil spirit leaped on them, mastered all[a] of them and overpowered them, so that they fled out of that house naked and wounded.

17 And this became known to all the residents of Ephesus, both Jews and Greeks. And fear fell upon them all, and the name of the Lord Jesus was extolled.

18 Also many of those who were now believers came, confessing and divulging their practices.

19 And a number of those who had practiced magic arts brought their books together and burned them in the sight of all. And they counted the value of them and found it came to fifty thousand pieces of silver.

20 So the word of the Lord continued to increase and prevail mightily.

Notice the Sons of Sceva had no relationship with God, yet they were still trying to do ministry. The consequences are self-explanatory. If it happened back then it will happen again. Again don't birth yourself out into any ministry, make sure you have the go ahead from God.

What if a person has more than one demon? Most people who are oppressed have more than one demon. That leads us back to the original text we read at the beginning this chapter.

Luke 8:26-33 (NKJV)

26 Then they sailed to the country of the Gadarenes,[a] which is opposite Galilee.

27 And when He stepped out on the land, there met Him a certain man from the city who had demons for a long time. And he wore no clothes,[b] nor did he live in a house but in the tombs.

28 When he saw Jesus, he cried out, fell down before Him, and with a loud voice said, "What have I to do with You, Jesus, Son of the Most High God? I beg You, do not torment me!"

29 For He had commanded the unclean spirit to come out of the man. For it had often seized him, and he was kept under guard, bound with chains and shackles; and he broke the bonds and was driven by the demon into the wilderness.

30 Jesus asked him, saying, "What is your name?"

And he said, "Legion," because many demons had entered him.

31 And they begged Him that He would not command them to go out into the abyss.

32 Now a herd of many swine was feeding there on the mountain. So they begged Him that He would permit them to enter them. And He permitted them.

33 Then the demons went out of the man and entered the swine, and the herd ran violently down the steep place into the lake and drowned.

A legion is a unit with 3000 to 6000 men. So Jesus cast out a man that had at least 3000 to 6000 demons in him. You may think that you could never do such a thing, then we have to consider what the scripture has to say about it.

John 14:12 (KJV)

12 Verily, verily, I say unto you, He that believeth on me, the works that I do shall he do also; and greater works than these shall he do; because I go unto my Father.

Luke 10:17-20 (KJV)

17 And the seventy returned again with joy, saying, Lord, even the devils are subject unto us through thy name.

18 And he said unto them, I beheld Satan as lightning fall from heaven.

19 Behold, I give unto you power to tread on serpents and scorpions, and over all the power of the enemy: and nothing shall by any means hurt you.

20 Notwithstanding in this rejoice not, that the spirits are subject unto you; but rather rejoice, because your names are written in heaven.

Jesus gives us clear instructions that what He did we can do at a greater level. You maybe think there is no way today a man can have 3000 to 6000 demons. You would be wrong. I have been in the room with a man that had legions of demons. Unfortunately, this individual like the woman I told you about earlier had no desire to be free and was committed to his demonic agenda.

You know you are dealing with someone who has more than one demon because the Holy Spirit will tell you. Or as you talk to them about their symptoms they will respond by saying "we" even though it is just you and the counselee in the room.

When it doubt use wisdom. If you don't feel comfortable don't do it. However, as a forewarning, you will be confronted with this type of ministry at some point. If it would be a help try to be trained or seek your own counsel to prepare yourself. I would also recommend by book, *Demons, Deliverance and Spiritual Warfare.*

There are many ministers who will train you in Deliverance Ministry. One of my favorite teachers is Apostle Ivory Hopkins; you can find many of his messages free on YouTube. Also be sure to support his ministry by purchasing many of his books and CD teachings, they are well worth it.

http://www.pilgrimsministry.org/

Never go into any ministry empty handed and unprepared. There is so much more that I can say about inner healing. There is also a workbook for individuals, a group facilitator workbook as well.

Chapter 12

The Root Of Rejection

Isaiah 53:3-4Living Bible (TLB)

3 We despised him and rejected him—a man of sorrows, acquainted with bitterest grief. We turned our backs on him and looked the other way when he went by. He was despised, and we didn't care.

4 Yet it was our grief he bore, our sorrows that weighed him down. And we thought his troubles were a punishment from God, for his own sins!

We cannot leave without talking about rejection. Rejection is a bitter root. When rejection continues to fester it will cause long lasting effects. When a person is still hurt from the long term effects of rejection, they will then begin to reject the thing that God has purposed for their lives. Fear of rejection will cause you to miss divine moments and divine connections. What if God is sending the spouse of your dreams, but your spirit of rejection caused you to miss that the thing that God has for you? You can have a great opportunity right in front of your face but the root of rejection will cause you to miss it.

Within the counseling session, you must learn when a counselee is struggling with the root of rejection.

Rejection simply means to be refused. It means to be denied. Rejection means to refuse to accept, consider, submit to, take for some purpose. Let's be honest rejection hurts; no one wants to be rejected. No one wants to be rejected at any level, yet we all have experienced rejection at some point and time. Even God Himself has experienced rejection from His people. There is no need to run from rejection; rather we must have a clear understanding of who were are, our identity in God and his love towards us.

We have a Father who doesn't just sit and look at our plight, but He understands it. I said something that is worth repeating, and that is God Himself was rejected. We will talk more about rejection that manifest in our client's in a minute.Let us look at rejection from the kingdom of God's perspective. When Jesus walked the earth, He often told stories, called parables to explain the kingdom of God. In the text that we will read, Jesus was explaining rejection.

Matthew 21:33-42Living Bible (TLB)

33 "Now listen to this story: A certain landowner planted a vineyard with a hedge around it, and built a platform for the watchman, then leased the vineyard to some farmers on a sharecrop basis, and went away to live in another country.

34 "At the time of the grape harvest he sent his agents to the farmers to collect his share.

35 But the farmers attacked his men, beat one, killed one, and stoned another.

36 "Then he sent a larger group of his men to collect for him, but the results were the same.

37 Finally the owner sent his son, thinking they would surely respect him.

38 "But when these farmers saw the son coming, they said among themselves, 'Here comes the heir to this estate; come on, let's kill him and get it for ourselves!'

39 So they dragged him out of the vineyard and killed him.

40 "When the owner returns, what do you think he will do to those farmers?"

41 The Jewish leaders replied, "He will put the wicked men to a horrible death and lease the vineyard to others who will pay him promptly."

42 Then Jesus asked them, "Didn't you ever read in the Scriptures: 'The stone rejected by the builders has been made the honored cornerstone;[a] how remarkable! What an amazing thing the Lord has done'?

We have already read in Isaiah how Jesus was rejected not only was He rejected he was despised. Despise means to feel a strong dislike for someone or something that you think is bad or worthless.

So the story in Matthew is about God the father, and His son Jesus. God sent prophets and priest to bring the people of God back to Him in relationship. They killed and persecuted the ones He sent. So God sent His son Jesus. Jesus was foretelling of His death. Guess what they did to God's son? Jesus is telling us in the text what will happen. We now know that Jesus was murdered. We know he rose again. However look at the ending of the text verse 42. The same one they have rejected has been the most honored cornerstone.

The same one that they rejected is the foundation for all life. The most important person that has ever been was rejected by the very ones He was trying to save.

At the beginning of the chapter, we read how Jesus was despised and rejected. Many scholars believe that Jesus was rejected long before He went to the cross, but also in childhood. There are reports that he never got along with children His age. He was isolated and strange. He was also known to be a bastard child. Meaning it was well known by the time Joseph and Mary got married that Joseph was not his biological father. Mary was showing and at least four months pregnant when she comes back into town from her sabbatical with her cousin Elizabeth. Again none of this was confirmed. Imagine the rumors that were spread about Mary and Joseph. This was not like today where many children are born out of wedlock.

It is thought that he didn't have a close relationships with his siblings. You don't really see him hanging out with his biological family other than his mother. One brother didn't get saved until Jesus had died. I believe Jesus was rejected long before His public ministry began.

It is important to note that rejection is a season of test that God ordains for anyone called to ministry. You must past the test of rejection. Every leader within the bible had a season of rejection. You name it (Abraham, Moses, David, Joseph, Jesus) Rejection hurts when it comes from people that we are trying to help, or from people we love the most. Don't worry we are still talking about inner healing I am giving you the foundation before we move forward.

Matthew 22:1-14 (TLB)

22 1-2 Jesus told several other stories to show what the Kingdom of Heaven is like.

"For instance," he said, "it can be illustrated by the story of a king who prepared a great wedding dinner for his son.

3 Many guests were invited, and when the banquet was ready, he sent messengers to notify everyone that it was time to come. **But all refused!**

 4 So he sent other servants to tell them, 'Everything is ready and the roast is in the oven. Hurry!'

5 "But the guests he had invited merely laughed and went on about their business, one to his farm, another to his store;

6 others beat up his messengers and treated them shamefully, even killing some of them.

7 "Then the angry king sent out his army and destroyed the murderers and burned their city.

8 And he said to his servants, 'The wedding feast is ready, and the guests I invited aren't worthy of the honor.

9 Now go out to the street corners and invite everyone you see.'

10 "So the servants did, and brought in all they could find, good and bad alike; and the banquet hall was filled with guests.

11 But when the king came in to meet the guests, he noticed a man who wasn't wearing the wedding robe provided for him.[a]

12 "'Friend,' he asked, 'how does it happen that you are here without a wedding robe?' And the man had no reply.

13 "Then the king said to his aides, 'Bind him hand and foot and throw him out into the outer darkness where there is weeping and gnashing of teeth.'

14 For many are called, but few are chosen."

The story is again the story of the relationship between God and Israel. They repeatedly rejected God's invitation to divine relationship with Him. Notice the similarities in the text the Father prepared the wedding for his son. The analogy is that God is the Father in the text and Jesus is His son. Once Israel rejected God's invitation to relationship with Him, that opened the door for gentiles to come and have communion with Him.

I want you to think about it. Have you ever gone to a wedding? What about your wedding? We know the story is about a rich king, so this wasn't any thrown together party. Imagine being a king putting on a big wedding reception with all the fixings and no one comes. Or even worse someone comes, but they don't even think so much of your wedding that they show up with jeans and a t-shirt on. How would you feel? That is what happened. Being called is one thing being chosen is another. When the father bids us to come, we must respond to his invitation.

God doesn't like being rejected, yet He has been rejected from the beginning of time, and neither do we. If we belong to God we will be rejected.

What needs to happen is not that we pray not to be rejected but our perspective on rejection changes. If you see rejection as God preparing you for the greater than you are doing good. Most people don't understand the kingdoms perspective of rejection.

The counselees that you see don't view rejection from the kingdom's view. They don't see that God had them to be different so He can usher them into the extraordinary. When we don't submit our rejection to the foot of the cross, it becomes a root of bitterness that rejection then takes roots and grows. Sometimes the fruit of rejection is so settle we don't always see it.

I was telling my client's today you know a person's root by their fruit. You know an apple tree because the fruit is an apple. You know an orange tree because of the orange fruit. You know what seed has been planted based upon what fruit it bears. You know that rejection is present when you see the fruit.

Let's look at the fruit of rejection.

1. When a person isolates.
2. Inability to communicate. When a person cannot communicate they secretly fear if they speak up even when they are being mistreated they will be rejection.
3. Attention seeking behaviors or they are very clingy.
4. Any person that needs constant reassuring is struggling with the root of rejection.
5. Being easily offended.
6. Overly concerned about how people will perceive this. Often these people suffer from depression and anxiety because they isolate and worry.
7. Perfectionism.
8. Overachieving, (performance driven) this individual is always working towards excellence to seek approval.
9. Constantly complaining.
10. Inability to receive critic.
11. Believes no one understands them.
12. Having to prove oneself.

12. Anyone who is abusive suffers from a history of rejection.

13. A history of broken relationships. If everywhere you go there is some drama, and you are the common denominator, you maybe the problem.

14. Difficulty is cultivating authentic relationships.

15. Inability to take a compliment.

16. Inability to be emotionally intimidate with someone.

17. Surface conversations. These people never go deep in conversation because of fear.

18. Keeping people at an emotional distance for fear of rejection.

As stated when someone struggles with the fear of rejection it can be camouflaged as something else. The person may not know that they are struggling with a root of rejection.

In fact, I recently met with someone who was a high ranking government official. He had accomplished a lot and had a level of notoriety, yet he struggled with depression and anxiety. As we talked what I came to understand was that even with all his accomplishments what he was struggling with was a root of rejection. His rejection led him to be an overachiever. There is nothing wrong with pushing yourself and being highly motivated. But subconsciously this individual was an overachiever because of the root of rejection in his childhood.

Let's consider another example:

John is 30 year old male. John saw a beautiful woman who we will call Alicia. Alicia was 30 years old, poised, educated, a Christian and beautiful. John has never been married before. He has always wanted a wife and children. John prayed and prayed, and when he met Alicia, he thought she was an answer to prayers. Alicia, however, had previously been married for five years and divorced. Her marriage started off beautifully; she trusted her husband explicitly. She and her then husband together made plans for a life together. They wanted to have children, build a legacy; they wanted to be a power couple, nothing missing nothing broken. Alicia's plans of a great future with her husband ended when she discovered him in bed with another man. There she was five years with a man, no children, now no marriage and what she called a waste of time.

Alicia was a Christian. Eventually, she knew that she had to forgive and move on. So that is what she did, or at least that is what she thought she did. This is when John comes into the picture.

When they meet, John is kind, caring and loving. He is genuinely a great guy. Alicia was guarded when she met him, but she could see the goodness in him. John thought Alicia was quite a woman, and he knew he wanted to spend the rest of his life with her. Alicia was not so sure. Alicia knew that John was a great guy, he would make a great husband, he was kind, hardworking, handsome and caring but she just didn't feel for him the way he felt for her.

However her friends and family convinced her that she would be crazy if she didn't start seeing John. Eventually, they started dating after Alicia let her guard down some, John quickly let his feelings be known, she was still trying to convince herself. She had some second thoughts, but considering what she had been through, she assumed that her guard was up due to her ex-husband's infidelity.

They continued the relationship for a few years. They even got engaged. Alicia had plans to go to medical school and become a doctor. John was well established in his career as an accountant and supported her dreams. Everyone around Alicia thought they made a wonderful couple. People around her praised her and God for redeeming her considering what she had been through. Alicia was still guarded and unsure. John noticed how guarded Alicia was but decided to be persistent he had determined to win her heart.

John was a great person, but Alicia realized that he wasn't a great person for him. Just because he was a nice guy and a Christian doesn't mean they were meant to be together as husband and wife. He was a great friend, a shoulder to lean on, but he wasn't her type of guy. After a few years of dating, she realized that he was a great guy but not what God had ordained for his life or hers for that matter.

John had made plans to marry her. Alicia decided that she didn't want to get married. She had gotten accepted into medical school. Alicia had made up in her mind that she didn't want to be in a relationship with John. Her feelings had not changed, in fact, while visiting the school she had met a wonderful man that had the same core values as hers. Although they had never dated, they were colleagues. They initially were friends. Until one day he made his intentions known to her that he was interested but he made it clear that he was not that guy and wound not pursue her because she was already in a relationship with another guy.

Alicia knew instantly what she wanted to do. She realized that she just didn't have the same feelings for John even before she met her fellow med school colleague. She knew he was a good guy, but he wasn't for her.

John, on the other hand, knew that Alicia was distant, but he always attributed it to her experience in her previous marriage. He assumed that she would change eventually. His family and friends kept giving him sound advice. They told him that she was a good person, but it wasn't a God ordained match. He didn't listen. At this point, John was in his thirties, and he wanted to get married.

Eventually, Alicia had no choice but to break it to John. She told him that he was a great guy, but she wasn't for him. John was devastated. He wanted to work it out with Alicia, but she wouldn't budge. She maintained her boundaries with him. Eventually she moved away to school. She stopped returning his phone calls, or attempts to meet up with her. She began dating the other guy, and in a year she was engaged. John was devastated. John was still single, hurt and felt as if he had wasted his time.

John realized that he made a mistake of making Alicia his first love instead of God. John realized that he had become guilty of idolatry. He idolized Alicia. He hated that she found someone so quickly and was getting married because he thought that she would be his wife. Eventually, he did see that she wasn't the one for him. He realized that he was a good guy, but he and Alicia were not a match made in heaven. As he thought about the relationship, he realized that they had different core values. He was good at saving money; she was good at spending it. He loved a nice evening at home; she liked going out. He was Pentecostal Christian; she was more conservative. He loved spending time with family; she didn't have a large family so always being around his family wasn't her thing. He often went to family gatherings alone without her. He was in ministry she never supported his ministry engagements. He was a giver; she wasn't a helper. He realized this all after the relationship was over. He realized that he had allowed his idolatry of her to cloud his judgement. He couldn't see what was there. She was a good person, but they were not good for each other.

John eventually forgave, but he still desired to be married. Eventually, John repented for making Alicia his idol. Alicia moved on and was happy in medical school. John focused on his career and ministry. Eventually, John was introduced to a lovely young lady named Caring while at church. Caring was just like her name. She was an elementary school teacher. She was working towards getting her master's degree. Caring loved the Lord and was waiting on God for a man.

John instantly could see she had a beautiful spirit. Caring was guarded but not in the way Alicia was guarded. Caring knew who she was and was determined not to compromise her standards. She wanted a man of God that loved God more than her. She wanted a man of God that could lead her. She wanted a man of God that God had ordained for her life.

After exchanging numbers John and Caring talked on the phone. They knew that God ordained this. After hanging up the phone they both individually prayed, they sought wise counsel from their parents and leaders. Things seemed to be going in a great direction. John would often be distant. He would go days without calling her. When he did call her he seemed distant for surface conversation, it almost like he was afraid to get close to Caring. Caring wasn't sure what was going on with John she thought they were doing well and was hopefully, that they would have a great future.

Caring was a woman of worth and value. All she knew was that John had better get it together or she would be done with him.

I know that was a long story, but we must dissect it. There are several points of rejection. I gave you this more complicated example because it shows how rejection manifests itself in ways we don't initially see. Before I give you the answers, I want you to discuss the pressures points.

Where in the text did you find rejection?

What were the effects of rejection that each experienced within the text?

If you were Alicia's counselor where would you begin?

If you were John's counselor where would you begin?

Answer:

Alicia's had experienced rejection from the man she loved her husband. Because she had experienced rejection, it did make her cold towards John. Rhe spirit of rejection also clouded her judgement. She wasn't able to initially see that John wasn't for her because of the hurt she still felt from the betrayal of her husband. The fruit of rejection also made Alicia second guess herself. Alicia had a feeling that John wasn't for her, but she kept second guessing it because she wasn't sure that her feelings were not more related to her previous relationship. Self-doubt is always a sign of rejection. Rejection causes you to second guess yourself or not be certain of who you are.

John was another one that dealt with rejection. John wasn't sure of himself, so he pursued someone who didn't have the same core values as him. Believe it or not when you feel the spirit of rejection you tend to put up with something that is not for you because you feel as though you can't do any better. John probably thought that Alicia was such a great catch he couldn't do any better, even though she appeared not to be his type. She was a Christian, but the reality was they had nothing in common. Had he not already been dealing with a spirit of rejection before even meeting Alicia He would have seen her beauty but knew he wasn't for her.

Rejection makes a person keep people at a distance for fear of getting hurt. Because John had experienced rejection when God did finally place His God ordained mate in front of him, he didn't see it. Caring was who John had prayed for yet he couldn't see what was plainly there. John was distant because he was afraid of getting hurt again. Caring knew her worth and value as a woman and refused to run after John. Caring was right, if John didn't get his act together, she would be done with him, and he still would be waiting for a spouse. Again when a person has experienced a season of rejection, they keep people at a distance for fear of getting hurt again.

The reality is Caring could not heal John's wounds. She wasn't their when he was hurt so she shouldn't have the repercussions of his spirit of rejection.

John is in your office, where do you begin.

Of course you want to ask about the female relationships in his life. When a man is broken and distant in relationships there are entry points? Either the entry point is his mother or a female that he had in his life. We don't know about John's mother. We could ask about why he became so attached to this woman so quick and inquire about roots related to his mother. We did identify a root rejection point was that he gave his heart to the wrong woman. She wasn't a bad woman; she wasn't the woman for him.

When an individual is guilt of idolatry (idol worship), there is a root of rejection present because they are looking for validation outside of God being the source.

This was just an example we could have discussed different examples such as mother wounds and father wounds, career rejection, etc.

The next question we must answer is how do we minister healing to someone who has experienced the fruit of rejection?

The first thing we must understand is that you can't get free from what you don't acknowledge. We have said this before. If a person is in denial about their feelings or if they are repressing them it is not going to work.

When counseling the individual, you would want to point out to them that they are struggling with the fruit of rejection. You would also want to point out where. Even though it may be obvious to you, it may not be obvious to them. For example, in the case of John, he may not be able to identify that he is struggling with rejection. He may just think of it as a lesson learned, he may not understand that his coldness towards Caring is a direct result of his broken heart with Alicia.

I want to clarify I am not suggesting that there be no balance. I am not suggesting that John's behavior towards Caring should be the same as when he first met Alicia. He has learned to use discernment and wisdom. But if his actions are motivated by fear and not love then the fruit of rejection is involved.

After you identify the fruit of rejection, remember there can be more than one place. For example, if John had a bad childhood, then he was rejected at school then he was rejected in previous relationships, our interaction in the counseling session should specify all of that.

Then after we identify where the breech was, we have to again talk to the counselee about forgiveness and repentance. He must forgive the Alicia. Now in the case of John he said he had forgiven, but in actuality, his actions proved otherwise. Then the counselee must repent before God because he failed to obey God's voice. You may say how did God speak to him? When his family and parents were giving him wise counsel about the previous relationship with Alicia believe it or not that was God speaking through them to him. God can speak to us in an audible voice, but often he sends leaders and other people that have our heart to give us wise counsel. Yes John was a good guy, but he wasn't listening

John 10:5 KJV

My sheep know my voice and the voice of a stranger they will not the follow.

John was following his flesh, his voice and not the voice of God.

We must continue to minister the heart of a father to the counselee. This is where the cognitive behavioral therapy comes in. Have the counselee write down all faulty thinking patterns that they have about themselves and the world. Then in session, we must compare that to the word of God to their faulty thought patterns.

We have to identify where the faulty beliefs are. As we identify them, we pray against the faulty beliefs. We then have to replace the faulty beliefs with the word of God.

Again before we leave let us review I have given you a lot of information. We must first identify that the individual is struggling with the fruit of rejection. We then must identify the causes of the rejection. Then we identify how it is negatively affecting a person's life. We must also teach the individual about the effect of rejection because they may not be aware that they are struggling with the effect of rejection.

We must teach them how to identify faulty thinking patterns. We must teach them how to replace the thoughts with the word of God. We must walk them through the journey of forgiveness. We must also teach them how to embrace the Father God's love. When you are clear about the love of God, you won't struggle with the negative effects of God.

When a person has the fruit of rejection, they are not clear about their identify in God. In fact, most of the inner healing counselee's struggle with some fruit of rejection and are not clear about their identify in God. They often take on the spirit of an orphan otherwise known as an orphan spirit because they are not certain and affirmed in the foundation of the Father's love.

Think about what an orphan is. An orphan is a child who has no parents, or their parents are dead. Imagine going through life feeling as if no one wants you; you are not loved. The individual may not be an orphan naturally, but they have an orphan spirit. When we counsel others, we must assist them in understanding that God loves them, that they have his very nature. They belong to Him. When you know that God loves you the spirit of rejection cannot rest in that individual.

I want to make it clear it is not that we won't experience rejection, we will. People won't like you for some reason. Maybe they think you are too fat, to skinny, to bold, to quiet. Whatever when a person is affirmed in the love of the father, they see it but it doesn't devastate them.

I was interacting with someone a couple of weeks ago. To be honest, I don't experience rejection in my adult life as much as an I did when I was a child because at this point in my life I have accomplished so much, most people when they do speak of me speak very highly of me. This person basically in so many words rejected me. Still, because I am affirmed in my father God's love it didn't devastate me. I just realized that I am not for everyone. Nothing wrong with that.

In ministry, in life, that is just life. Everyone is not going to like you. As much as I want everyone to like what I write there are some that don't. It doesn't mean I am not good at what I do. That is how you know you don't have the fruit of rejection; you just see things as they are and you move forward. We don't have to be bound by the opinion of other people. We have to be clear about who we are in God.

I know I am beautiful. I know I am a great writer. I know I am a woman who walks in integrity, spiritual authority and virtue. I am not bragging, but I know who I am, I found myself in God. When I am clear about who I am the opinions of other people, don't matter.

So we have to explore with our counselee's the root of rejection. Again the root of rejection is connected to bitterness, resentment, unforgiveness. Roots of rejection should be dealt with from the very beginning of the counseling sessions and as well as throughout the sessions.

Well, my fellow workers of Christ, our time is just about up for now. There is so much more that I could say but we must end for now. We have not talked about how when a person has a "hero" complex it is rooted in rejection. We have not talked in detail how this presents itself in our Christian leaders and persons in the human services field.

Nevertheless, if there is one thing that I will always remember my pastor taught me that even every greater preacher must know when to close or stop. He told us how just because you are done doesn't mean you are out of the word. You have to teach, then learn when to stop. Trust me this is my passion; I could go on even now my mind is thinking about what next. This is just a starting place. I hope that the words you have read here have helped you in some way to further your counseling ministry.

Our journey together for this book ends, but our journey together as fellow co-labors in Christ does not. As a part of this book series there is a training manual for counselors, a group curriculum for those who want to use the tools in group settings, there is an individual workbook for counselee's who identify that they need inner healing work. The individual workbook is not a replacement for working in session with a counselor but a supplement. The journal workbook can be used as a standalone journal but it is highly recommended that the counselee use the workbook in conjunction with counseling sessions. Remember I said you do want to give the counselee something to go home with some kind of therapeutic homework.

Also, something to keep in mind is that the training manual incorporates a section on how to do inner healing work with children and families. We also will continue to address inner healing work within couples.

Also, I am holding training seminars on how to implement inner healing work for other counselors, churches leaders, and Christian layperson. If you would like to request me to speak or offer training for your people, please feel free to get in touch with me. My contact information will be available at my website:www.samariacolbert.com

God bless you.

I end this book with the same scripture we started with, this is or mandate, this is what we have been anointed, called and commissioned to do. Please never forget it.

Isaiah 61:1-3 (KJV)

1 The Spirit of the Lord God is upon me; because the Lord hath anointed me to preach good tidings unto the meek; he hath sent me to bind up the brokenhearted, to proclaim liberty to the captives, and the opening of the prison to them that are bound;

2 To proclaim the acceptable year of the Lord, and the day of vengeance of our God; to comfort all that mourn;

3 To appoint unto them that mourn in Zion, to give unto them beauty for ashes, the oil of joy for mourning, the garment of praise for the spirit of heaviness; that they might be called trees of righteousness, the planting of the Lord, that he might be glorified.

Chapter 13

Bonus:

The Case For Christian Counseling

Psalm 1:1 (KJV)

1 Blessed is the man that walketh not in the counsel of the ungodly, nor standeth in the way of sinners, nor sitteth in the seat of the scornful.

Okay, one final bit of information. In my journey as a counselor, I have come across other Christians including ministers who don't understand that counseling is a ministry. I have also come across individuals who experience stigma related to seeking out any form of counseling. Attached is a chapter from another book that you will find helpful for yourself and others as you demystify false beliefs related to seeking out a counselor.

Inevitably you will meet someone who doesn't understand the counseling ministry. In fact even after being in the field over 11 years doing this work, when I get asked by other ministers what ministry I am in, I tell them the counseling ministry they look at me strange. People to this day don't understand that ministry of counseling. Ironically we wonder why we have so many pastors and leaders committing suicide, but some still don't understand. My mission is not to convince hardened hearts; I don't argue with people about why my ministry that God anointed me for is a valid ministry, there are too many scriptures to validate the ministry.

However there maybe someone who needs the ministry of inner healing counseling, maybe you need to be reassured within yourself that counseling is justified by scripture. Maybe you need to have a heart to heart with a potential counselee who is guarded in your office because they won't want to appear "unchristian like." Attached is a copy of a chapter from another book entitled: Deliverance From Depression, it makes a case for Christian Counseling. Pull this chapter out, show it to your counselee, you can even go over some of the scriptures together. There is no denying that God's hands are on the ministry of the counselor and we need to be utilized more within local churches. Isn't it ironic that you have so many ministries within the church, single's ministry, marriage ministry, men's ministry, women's ministry but the ministry of the counselor is still left out in many of our local churches? The type of counseling ministry we do cannot be done by your pastor alone; it needs its own department within the church. We have to keep praying for change.

Bonus Chapter: Deliverance From Depression

Psalm 1:1-3 (NKJV)

1 Blessed is the man

Who walks not in the counsel of the ungodly,

Nor stands in the path of sinners,

Nor sits in the seat of the scornful;

2 But his delight is in the law of the Lord,

And in His law he meditates day and night.

3 He shall be like a tree

Planted by the rivers of water,

That brings forth its fruit in its season,

Whose leaf also shall not wither;

And whatever he does shall prosper.

I could not go any further into depression without the importance of emphasizing to you the reader, why

Christian counseling and therapy is a necessity to your full deliverance. It is important that we set the foundation; by dispelling myths about this issue while explaining the facts.

There are many things that we have embraced in the church to be God's laws, thoughts, or commands when they are not. Man has taken its own culture and made it appear as God's. For example, when I was going through school, I realized at some point, that I had an anointing to counsel and work with individuals who suffer from mental health issues. I remember sitting in church one day and hearing the minister say, "you don't need a counselor, you need Jesus." I can remember other times being in a church where a man talked about how "you don't need to come to see a therapist and sit in someone's office for 50 minutes to get your deliverance." And on he went. The inner conflict that I felt was that, how can I be blood washed, spirit filled Christian, that operates in spiritual gifts, is called to deliverance ministry and want to be a therapist? Casting out demons is what I am supposed to be doing. Eventually, I figured the reality is, I could do both.

Myth #1

Christians are not supposed to seek mental health counseling from a therapist. All they need is to go to an alter and have someone lay hands on them.

This is not true! In fact, there is no scripture that says, "You are not supposed to seek out counseling or that it is sin to go to therapy." I always say there is no need to add on commandments or scripture that don't exist. To the contrary, scripture tells us that we are supposed to seek wise counsel.

I remember hearing from a woman who had sought out marriage counseling after she was having some difficulty in her marriage. She said she felt so bad about that and reported that she had to repent. Not because of the difficulties in her marriage. She was repenting and asking God for forgiveness for going to see a therapist. That is absolute foolishness. I am not God, but it is silly and downright foolish not to seek out counseling, particularly for marriage. Maybe more Christians wouldn't be getting divorced so soon if they had participated in marriage counseling, even after marriage, and definitely before marriage.

Fact: Christians are supposed to seek out wise counsel.

Proverbs 20:5 (NKJV) Counseling in the heart of a man is like deep water, but a man with understanding draws it out.

Proverbs 20:18 (NKJV) Plans are established by counsel: By wise counsel wage war

Proverbs 1:5 (NKJV)….And a man of understanding will obtain wise counsel

Proverbs 3:32 (NKJV) But His secret counsel is with the upright

Proverbs 4:5 (NKJV) Get wisdom, get understanding

Proverbs 8:14 (NKJV) Counsel is mine and sound wisdom;

Proverbs 11:14 (NKJV) Where there is no counsel people fall. But in the multitude of counselors there is safety

Proverbs 12:25 (NKJV) Anxiety in the heart of man causes depression, But a good word makes glad.

Proverbs 15:22 (NKJV)Without counsel, plans go awry, But in the multitude of counselors they are established

Proverbs 19:20, 21(NKJV) Listen to counsel and receive instruction that you may be wise in your latter days. There are many plans in a man's heart, nevertheless the Lord's counsel will stand

Proverbs 24:6 (NKJV) For by wise counsel, you will wage your own war; And in a multitude of counselors there is safety.

Proverbs 27:9 (NKJV) Ointment and perfume delight the heart, And the sweetness of a man's friend gives delight by hearty counsel.

Psalm 1:1 (NKJV)

1 Blessed is the man

Who walks not in the counsel of the ungodly,

Nor stands in the path of sinners,

Nor sits in the seat of the scornful;

Don't allow the ungodly to counsel you. So if you are going to seek out counsel, make sure it's by a Christian, preferably, a licensed mental health professional and a Christian.

The point is, God not only says that it is perfectly fine to seek counseling, He expects it. God didn't put any conditions on it. Counseling is counseling.

Myth 2: The only person who is supposed to counsel you is your pastor.

Although it is true that often times, pastors may have some training or anointing to counsel, it comes along with the position. To my dismay, often pastors have very little training in the counseling profession; they have little to no training in the specific areas of mental health counseling or inner healing counseling. There is no specific scripture that says the only person who is supposed to counsel you is the pastor. I am a licensed therapist who also is a spirit filled believer. In my experience, it is better to seek counsel from a licensed, trained counselor.

Myth 3: It is possible to obtain emotional healing absent from Christ.

This is false. As a trained professional I did not go to some Christian school or have any official training from a Christian school of learning. The formal education I gained was from secular schools, although they were good schools. The world's system always tries to get some healing absent from Christ. In fact, most schools of higher learning do not even acknowledge the spiritual world or how one's spirit being is impacted emotional health.

Truth:

Healing absent from Christ is only temporary. My frustration as I have gone through my career is simple. We aren't helping people; we aren't getting to the cause or true healing. The world systems only put band aides on deep rooted wounds. We are taught to change behavior, so a person may walk away from the counseling session feeling better or stopping a certain problematic behavior, but it always comes back. There was no true deliverance. That's why if therapists would be honest, we see the same clients come in and out the door. The ones who have real and lasting changes are the ones who are Christians. Trust me; what I am saying is the truth. Again, I am not just some preacher sitting behind a pulpit talking about it. I see it every day. In my career, I have worked in mental health hospitals, managed care companies, and in private practice counseling people. Although, I do not regret my experiences; I believe that everywhere I have been was so that God could prepare me to walk in what I want to do. Nonetheless, counseling and healing outside of Christ is a revolving door, you may leave the counselors office with some life change, but you will be back.

That does not negate the need to seek to counsel, again it must be by a Christian counselor, and Christ must be the center of the therapy session.

My private practice was started after years of working for others. Kingdom Creative Counseling is a Christian practice, specific for individuals who have experienced all kinds of mental health, spiritual and demonic oppression. I have a heart to work with individuals who have survived early childhood sexual assault. I also work with children. If you are a therapist who is in private practice or desires to make Christ the center then your practice will flourish

Myth #4: You don't need to seek to counsel.

Truth: The reality is, just because you don't go to seek out a counselor, doesn't mean you don't need to go. You can technically live your entire life and never brush your teeth, that doesn't mean you don't need to do so. Everyone at some point and time in their life should go to a counselor. Engaged couples should **ALWAYS** seek out pre-marriage counseling, regardless of how much you think you heard from God. The reality is, there is still so much stigma attached to seeking out a therapist. I have clients who show up to my office and say, "I am not crazy." No, they are wise. I think it is a cowardly person who sits at home by themselves and suffers when God has provided anointed godly people to help. You can be healed by yourself and never seek out help, but why would you want to? That is a pride issue.

Myth #5: If I seek out a counselor, then they will tell other's my business.

Truth: A licensed counselor is governed by the federal HIPPA laws, laws that protect confidentiality and their license. Any information you disclose of in a counselors office is considered strictly confidential and cannot be released to anyone. If anyone tries to ask the counselor about the session, the counselor literally can't even acknowledge you as a client in their agency. The only limitation to that is if the client discloses of intent or plan to harm themselves or another. Any form of abuse. They must break the confidentiality agreement to protect the safety of themselves, the client or another.

Any information that you need to be released for whatever reason, a disclosure form is signed by you the client and specifically what is to be released. For example, even an emergency contact form, bringing someone that you want to a session, communicating with your insurance company, consent for release is signed first. If you don't sign, there is no releasing of information.

Myth: People in the bible never sat down with a counselor or therapist why should I?

Truth: This is false. Scripture tells us that the best therapist there was, was Jesus. He is called the wonderful counselor. However, there are many examples of people who sought counseling.

In fact, when you read the Old Testament, one of the functions of the prophet was to counsel. You see, countless Kings, Priests, and people in positions of authority seeking out the prophet. This is why one function for individuals who operate in the office of the prophet is to be a counselor. There are many examples of this in the bible, too many to name in this chapter. However, let us look at the example of Moses, a man who received wise counsel.

Exodus 18:1-27

The Message (MSG)

18 1-4 Jethro, priest of Midian and father-in-law to Moses, heard the report of all that God had done for Moses and Israel, his people, and the news that God had delivered Israel from Egypt. Jethro, Moses' father-in-law, had taken in Zipporah, Moses' wife who had been sent back home, and her two sons. The name of the one was Gershom (Sojourner) for he had said, "I'm a sojourner in a foreign land"; the name of the other was Eliezer (God's-Help) because "The God of my father is my help and saved me from death by Pharaoh."

5-6 Jethro, Moses' father-in-law, brought Moses his sons and his wife there in the wilderness where he was camped at the mountain of God. He had sent a message ahead to Moses: "I, your father-in-law, am coming to you with your wife and two sons."

7-8 Moses went out to welcome his father-in-law. He bowed to him and kissed him. Each asked the other how things had been with him. Then they went into the tent. Moses told his father-in-law the story of all that God had done to Pharaoh and Egypt in helping

Israel, all the trouble they had experienced on the journey, and how God had delivered them.

9-11 Jethro was delighted in all the good that God had done for Israel in delivering them from Egyptian oppression. Jethro said, "Blessed be God who has delivered you from the power of Egypt and Pharaoh, who has delivered his people from the oppression of Egypt. Now I know that God is greater than all gods because he's done this to all those who treated Israel arrogantly."

12 Jethro, Moses' father-in-law, brought a Whole-Burnt-Offering and sacrifices to God. And Aaron, along with all the elders of Israel, came and ate the meal with Moses' father-in-law in the presence of God.

13-14 The next day Moses took his place to judge the people. People were standing before him all day long, from morning to night. When Moses' father-in-law saw all that he was doing for the people, he said, "What's going on here? Why are you doing all this, and all by yourself, letting everybody line up before you from morning to night?"

15-16 Moses said to his father-in-law, "Because the people come to me with questions about God. When something comes up, they come to me. I judge between a man and his neighbor and teach them God's laws and instructions."

17-23 Moses' father-in-law said, "This is no way to go about it. You'll burn out, and the people right along with you. This is way too much for you—you can't do this alone. Now listen to me. Let me tell you how to do this so that God will be in this with you. Be there for the people before God, but let the matters of concern be presented to God. Your job is to teach them the rules and instructions, to show them how to live, what to do. And then you need to keep a sharp eye out for competent men—men who fear God, men of integrity, men who are incorruptible—and appoint them as leaders over groups organized by the thousand, by the hundred, by fifty, and by ten. They'll be responsible for the everyday work of judging among the people. They'll bring the hard cases to you, but in the routine cases they'll be the judges. They will share your load and that will make it easier for you. If you handle the work this way, you'll have the strength to carry out whatever God commands you, and the people in their settings will flourish also."

24-27 Moses listened to the counsel of his father-in-law and did everything he said. Moses picked competent men from all Israel and set them as leaders over the people who were organized by the thousand, by the hundred, by fifty, and by ten. They took over the everyday work of judging among the people. They brought the hard cases to Moses, but in the routine cases they were the judges. Then Moses said good-bye to his father-in-law who went home to his own country.

Moses was and still is considered one of the greatest leaders that ever walked the earth. Yet here he is receiving counsel. The greater you become, the more it is a necessity that you seek out wise counseling.

This example dispels the myth that counseling is only for the poor and weak minded. Not so! If you want to be a great leader or are already in a position of leadership and authority, it is an absolute must that you have wise counsel. Not just yes people in your life. I found it interesting that of all the people Moses had around him, it was his father in law that gave him great counsel, someone who was not in his life on an ongoing daily basis.

It shows us that just because you have people around you, doesn't mean they are qualified to pour into your life. Seeking out a truly anointed, Christian counselor is not just about looking up someone in the yellow pages.

Counselors are people who walk in wisdom from God. They have the anointing of wisdom. Christian counselors have the gift of knowledge, wisdom; they can rightfully discern spirits, prophesy and they give clear instructions or directions. Although a great portion of counseling is more about listening, it also means to give direction.

I want to make it clear; we are to seek God first and foremost. Counselors, prophets, pastors whomever, they never are to operate in their anointing so much so that they replace the word of God for you. In fact, a good leader leads, they don't replace. They don't become the mouth piece of God for you! Not even the prophet, as some may believe. You have God on the inside, and you must seek Him first, not a man or woman! God leads, but counselors and leaders help to give direction; it is God who has the final say so.

In fact, years ago I was reading about this Christian therapist. He had just graduated with his master's degree and he began a practice in a small town. So his practice quickly started growing. People would come and get what they needed and go out. One day the

Holy Spirit spoke to him and said "don't give them everything."

The point is, leaders are to always lead you to the voice of God. In fact, when I was in undergrad, my favorite professor says, we professionally help people so that they become self-reliant. We don't help them, so they become dependent. Now as stated, I didn't go to a Christian school, but I got the revelation from that.

There is a wrong way to help people and a right way. You give them the tools that they need so that they don't have to come back to you every time they have an issue. We give people tools.

 One myth is that if you go to see a counselor, you must do so for the rest of your life. Although life does happen, if you are seeking a counselor, you should never be seeing the same counselor for years. This is an example of poor counseling. There is a beginning, middle, and end to counseling. You don't see the same counselor, for the same issue for years. Although much of my counseling is around issues of trauma, abuse, and takes much longer than one session, real counseling is not an overnight thing, but it still should not take years.

There is always progress. If you are not making progress, either you're going to the wrong counselor, or you are doing something wrong. A real Christian counselor doesn't counsel you so well that you become dependent on them, they counsel you, so you are reassured, confident, and become reliant on God, and His voice for your life. It is the same for any leader in your life. If they are insistent that you need them, and that you can't get to God any way but through them, then what you have is a controlling, Jezebel spirit. It may seem like a farce, but trust me when I tell you, I have seen this foolishness from the church. It is wrong and should never be!

The reality is, Christians deal with emotional and mental health issues like everyone else. In fact, sometimes more because they are going through demonic attacks. The attacks often come from our minds. The difference is we have hope, future, and Christ who is willing and able to deliver us. As I counsel non-Christians, many of them have a sense of hopelessness, because they think just because they suffer from something today, it will always be that way. A Christian can have the same issue, but they are confident that God is a healer and He will deliver. They know that although they don't like what they are going through right now, God is in control and he will intervene. The frequency, time frame, and duration of counseling, is much quicker for a Christian because the therapist and the counselee allow Christ and the Holy Spirit to do the work. However, that does not negate the need for a Christian counselor.

Tips to know when seeking out a counselor.

When you do find a contact, simply state that you are specifically looking for a Christian therapist. Christian counselors are in every state. You could go to www.findachristiancounselor.com

 or American Association of Christian Counselors Find a Counselor

www.aacc.net/resources/find-a-counselor/

Many licensed mental health professionals like myself are also credentialed with insurance companies. You can also call the 1-800 number on the back of your insurance card and ask for a someone who specializes in Christian counseling.

Also check out Psychology Today. You can select an option for a Christian Therapist, you can also put in your zip code to find the therapist that is closest to you. May counselors including myself advertise with Psychology Today.

www.psychologytoday.com

When seeking out a Christian counselor, there are certain criteria you want to look for are:

They should be licensed by an accredited institution of higher learning. All Christian's counselors should always have master's degrees and a license.

Do not seek a life coach or consultation for depression or any mental health issues. Although life coaches are beneficial, they are not qualified to handle major mental health issues.

If you are seeking counseling from someone who simply has a certificate, you run the risk of seeking counseling from someone who has very minimal training and not much experience. You can get a certificate to counsel or coach in a matter of months in some cases 3 months or less. A licensed counselor has to have at least 6 to 8 years of training minimally and experience before they can even get a license.

Make sure the counselor has a mental health background. Believe it, or not all Christians counsels have an understanding of mental health concerns.

This is so important even for inner healing work because a good counselor knows when to focus on mental health, versus inner healing. Every person may not be ready for inner healing work; they will be ready for mental health work.

Of course, you don't need a degree to counsel people that is what the anointing is for, but I am a firm believer that the anointing and preparation for any ministry are key. A licensed therapist is anointed, but again the preparation for the ministry of counseling is guaranteed, and you have a much better chance of getting what you need.

Remember there is the gift to counsel and there is the ministry to counsel. You want to seek counseling from someone who operates in both the gift and the ministry. That is what a licensed counselor guarantees.

Again seek counseling from someone who operates in the gift and the ministry to counsel.

Licensure should fall under one of the following categories: LCSW-Licensed Clinical Social Worker, LCCC- Licensed Clinical Christian Counselor, LCPC Licensed Clinical Professional Counselor, Licensed Psychologist (Psy D),

LCAS-Licensed Clinical Addictions Specialist. PsyD

Note, a certified life coach is not the same as a Christian Counselor; although in some instances a life coach can be beneficial in assisting to motivate you and give direction. For true inner healing and recovery, you should always seek a licensed Christian therapist.

Counseling by a licensed therapist guarantees confidentiality with the exception of harm to yourself and others.

It is always recommended that you seek godly counsel from a therapist who you do not have a personal relationship with, particularly in areas related to (childhood trauma, marriage, abuse issues).

In fact, I do not counsel family members or friends; this is considered a conflict of interest.

Although it is always helpful to seek out wise advice from someone you trust and can seek wisdom from. When you seek a Christian counselor, they are more concerned with the process of healing than the immediacy of healing. This is when you seek out counseling for a specific period over time. We always recommend no duel relationships so that the person offering counseling services can assist in a way that guarantees non bias.

You may want also to consider seeking counseling from someone who specializes in whatever area of counseling you are seeking assistance for. For example, my area of focus is childhood trauma, addictions, PTSD, abuse, so many of my clients are seeking counseling in that area.

If you are married seek out a counselor who specializes or has experience in marriage counseling.

Some say single people can't give marital counseling. However, Jesus and the Apostle Paul gave great instructions on the order, structure of marriage and neither of them married. The point is, I believe it is more important that the therapist be spirit led and know the principles of marriage by the bible standards.

Note that seeking pastoral counseling may be beneficial, however, confidentially is not guaranteed although it should be. You also run the risk of having your counseling session be somehow spoken about in the public view of your church, even if the pastor does not disclose your name. If you're okay with that, then it's your choice, but if you'd rather not hear other people hearing your story on Sunday morning, I recommend the alternative. As stated, although pastors have a great anointing to counsel, they most often have little to no understanding of mental health conditions.

My prayer is that we see more churches and Christians organizations offer a Christian counseling ministry by licensed mental health professionals.

Hopefully, I made the case. I encourage you to look at my website for other resources. God bless you and let us continue in the work of the Lord. I hope to see you at one of my seminars as we work together to advance the kingdom through the work of inner healing ministry.

Codependency. (n.d.) Retrieved from;
http://www.webmd.com/sex-
relationships/features/signs-of-a-codependent-
relationship#1

Covert Incest. (n.d.) Retrieved from;
https://www.goodtherapy.org/blog/emotional-covert-
incest-when-parents-make-their-kids-partners-
0914165

Defense Mechanism. (n.d.). Retrieved from
https://en.wikipedia.org/wiki/Defence_mechanisms

Defense Mechanism.(n.d.)
https://www.merriamwebster.com/dictionary/defense
%20mechanism.

Emotional Affair (emotional intimacy) (n.d.)
Retrieved from.
https://en.wikipedia.org/wiki/Emotional_affair

Emotional Incest. (n.d). Retrieved from
https://www.goodtherapy.org/blog/emotional-covert-
incest-when-parents-make-their-kids-partners-
0914165

Masking Personality. (n.d.). Retrieved from https://en.wikipedia.org/wiki/Masking_(personality)

Masking Personality. Retrieved from, https://en.wikipedia.org/wiki/Masking_(personality)

Maslow's Hiearch of Needs (n.d) Retrieved from. https://www.google.com/imgres?imgurl=https://www. simplypsychology.org/maslow.jpg&imgrefurl

Parentified Child Syndrome. (n.d.). Retrieved from; https://en.wikipedia.org/wiki/Parentification

Patterns and Pathologies. (2014, February 14). Retrieved from https://www.healyourlife.com/the-fabric-of-your-being. Vanzant, Iyvanla

Post Traumatic Stress Disorder. (n.d). Retrieved from https://en.wikipedia.org/wiki/Posttraumatic_embitter ment_disorder.

Post Traumatic Stress Disorder. (n.d.) Retrieved from https://en.wikipedia.org/wiki/Posttraumatic_embitter ment_disorder

South African Woman Forgives Murderer's Son (n.d). Retrieved July 1, 2015, http://www.geoffsshorts.blogspot.com

Unmet Emotional Needs. (n.d.) Retrieved from; Medical-dictionary.thefreedictionary.com/emotional+need-

7 Signs That You Have A Soul Tie. (n.d.). Retrieved from: http://krisvallotton.com/7-signs-of-an-unhealthy-soul-tie/. Vallotton.Kris.

The Cycle of Poverty. (n.d.). Retrieved from. https://en.wikipedia.org/wiki/Cycle_of_poverty

Woman Shows Incredible Mercy. (2011, June 8) Retrieved July 3, 2015, from ww.dailymail.co.uk.new/article-incredible-mercy-sons-killer-movies-door.htm.

About The Author:

Samaria was saved at eight years old. Shortly after that she received the baptism of the Holy Ghost. Samaria first received her call into ministry many years ago when attended to Bennett College in Greensboro, NC. After attending a youth-led Bible study, she learned that some things only come through fasting and prayer. The Lord impressed upon her to seek His face for what she needed to hear from Him. It was then that Samaria began to seek God for her purpose and destiny within the body of Christ. So after much prayer and fasting, God spoke to Samaria in a series of dreams and visions over a three year period. It was during this time that she experienced some of the greatest spiritual awakenings of her life. Her confidence in her relationship with God and His destiny for her life was certain.

Samaria Colbert is an anointed writer, licensed therapist, minister and consultant. She received her Bachelor's degree from Bowie State University, in Bowie, MD. She later went on to receive her Master's from Howard University, in Washington, D.C. She is currently pursuing a Ph.D. Samaria calls North Carolina home.

Samaria also has a heart to counsel; she is the founder and CEO of Kingdom Creative Counseling Services. The counseling part of her private practice is specifically for women, men, and children who have survived early childhood sexual abuse and domestic violence. Samaria uses an integrative approach to therapy that includes, mental health, inner healing, and deliverance, all biblically based so that complete healing and wholeness is achieved through Christ Jesus.

Samaria is also the founder and CEO of LIKEAPRO Professional Writing Services. An organization dedicated to a spirit of excellence and completing the writing projects for Christian professionals, lay persons, and fivefold ministers.

She believes in, "Absolute abandonment for the cost of the call of Jesus Christ." Samaria is a young woman, who loves God, loves His word, and is passionate above all about His purpose and destiny for her life.

Stay tuned, the future looks bright, and there is so much more to come from this dynamic, anointed and appointed a woman of God.

"What will you do in your lifetime that will have an impact on someone else's life for a lifetime?"

Samaria M. Colbert

To stay up to date with her latest writing projects, ministry and to request her to speak at your event please visit her website.

www.samariacolbert.com

www.likeaprowritingservices.com

Insurance accepted: BCBS of NC, Medicaid, Medicare, NCHC and out of pocket pay

336-543-0159

Depression

Christ Centered

Anxiety

Psychotic Disorders

Recovery from Early Child Sexual Abuse/Trauma

Domestic Violence   Recovery from Spiritual Abuse
Inner Healing and Deliverance

Play Therapy

Adults, Families, and Children Served

Thank You

Feel Free To Pick Up Other Inner Healing Resources:

Couches and Conversations Individual Workbook Journal

Couches and Conversations Group Manual

Couches and Conversations Clinicians Training Manual

www.samariacolbert.com

www.likeaprowritingservices.com

LikeAPro Professional Writing Services

<u>**Make sure you pick up your very own copy of Samaria's other books:**</u>

No Promise Without A Process The Makings Of A True Prophet

The Wisdom To Fulfilling Your Prophetic Destiny. A Memoir of Words, Warnings, And Pitfalls To Avoid Missing Your Prophetic Destiny.

This I know: Because There Are Choices You Make That Can Either Birth or Abort Your Spiritual Destiny

God Can Change Anyone

No Promise Without A Process The Makings Of A True Prophet Part II

Inside Out Because Real Transformations Happens From The Inside Out Not The Outside In

To Whom It May Concern

Wisdom, Warnings and Warfare

Hearing The Voice of God

Demons, Deliverance and Spiritual Warfare

Soul Ties

Not Without A Struggle

Trusting God Is Not Easy But It Is Worth It

Not Without A Purpose

Deliverance From Depression

No More Fear

You Are Not Forgotten

The Process of Emotional Healing

The Process of Emotional Healing Workbook

The Process of Emotional Healing Facilitators Guide

A Ready Made Writer

Hidden To Lead

Healing The Heart Through Forgiveness

The Ministry of Honor

Broken

Kingdom Mandates, Kingdom Mantles and Kingdom Authority

The Heart Of Worship

Restoration

Psychological Warfare

The Wait

The Wait Individual Workbook

The Wait Facilitators Guide

The Wait 60 Day Devotional

Let Down Your Nets

The Bible And Business

Who Beguiled You?

According To Your Faith

Couches and Conversations Workbook Journal

Couches and Conversations Group Manual

Couches and Conversations Training Manual

www.samariacolbert.com

www.likeaprowritingserviccs.com

www.samariacolbert.com

www.likeaprowritingservices.com

www.ingramcontent.com/pod-product-compliance
Lightning Source LLC
Chambersburg PA
CBHW070809280726
48660CB00015B/22